MEINHARD VON GERKAN (ED.)

PROJECTS IN CHINA

ARCHITECTS VON GERKAN, MARG AND PARTNERS

PRESTEL

Munich · Berlin · London · New York

CONTENTS

BUILDINGS AND PROJECTS

CHRONOLOGY

ESSAY

Impressions of the Far East
"My experiences of China"

I made my first visit to China in 1998 when I was invited to Beijing for the competition for a new building for the German School there. This was the only competition colloquium I have ever experienced that was attended by all those entering the competition. Clearly the interest in Beijing was enormous. The visit extended over a period of five days in December with temperatures of minus 25 degrees Celsius (minus 13 degrees Fahrenheit) and a wind blowing from across the Gobi Desert that was so ice cold that I allowed myself be persuaded to buy a fox-fur cap which turned out in fact to be made of rabbit. But it kept my head warm all the same. The visit to the Forbidden City, the excursion to the Great Wall made a lasting impression on me. I made a bet with my colleagues about when the school would be completed. We won the competition and the building was completed in a remarkably short time – and so I lost my bet. The stake of several bottles of red wine is still in storage in my cellar.

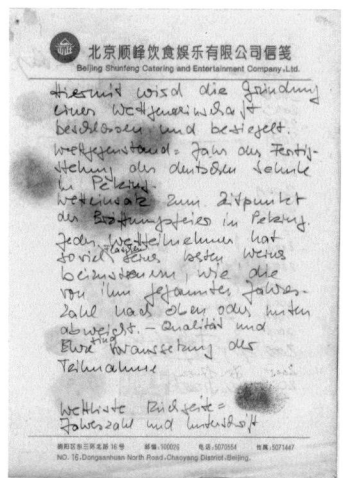 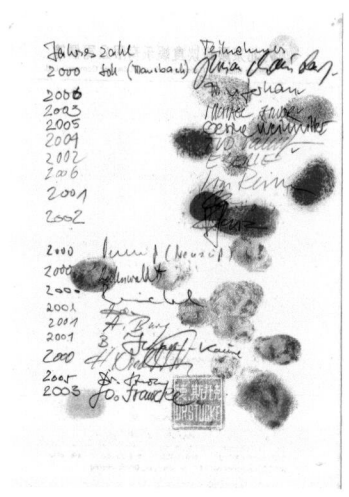

He bet, sealed and signed

Back then I did not recognize China's potential. I traveled to China quite innocently and was soon forced to concede that my ideas about this land as a developing country were very wrong. One could buy almost everything, there were more cars and fewer bicycles than I had expected, the hotels offered service of a European standard and there were a number of restaurants of the very highest quality. There was a great deal of demonstratively displayed wealth and pronounced luxury. The country was far more advanced than I had imagined. But at the time of my first visit to the country the idea that China could ever be a market for architecture and urban planning was non-existent.

The decisive turning point was a chance event that occurred two years later. The UIA Congress – the world meeting of architects – was held in Peking in Summer 1999 and I was invited to give a lecture there. A member of our office staff who knew a Chinese art student suggested organizing a gmp exhibition in Peking. The mother of this female student was a very influential figure in art circles in Beijing and she put an exhibition space in a famous museum at our disposal. We made our decisions at very short notice and as a consequence made a number of mistakes – for instance we had too much material and we had the drawings framed in Hamburg. But it turned out that transporting them, framed, by plane would be more expensive than having them framed in Peking. Therefore we had the frames removed and had the drawings framed again in Peking. The exhibition itself was a great success, also in the media, due in no small part to our host's contacts to important figures in the worlds of politics and the arts. There had never previously been an architecture exhibition in a museum; this was therefore something like an explosion in terms of public relations work. We were consequently able to build up a reputation as successful and reliable architects – whereas most of the other foreign offices functioned more as willing agents, i.e. they only did what was required of them. For a long time images of American Midwest architecture were dominant and were connected with decorative elements from the Chinese tradition, generally the end result looked like a kind of caricature. There was also a certain feeling of dissatisfaction in Chinese specialist circles about the Canadian, Japanese and French architecture offices. We represented an alternative position, so to speak. In China people are very open to new trends and we were initially regarded as a new trend. This was extremely beneficial and helped ensure that we were regularly invited to take part in competitions, even against competitors from America. The fact that we came with our own ideas was the basis for the position we have in China today. While not wishing to boast we can safely say we are the best-known foreign architecture office there. In the specialist Chinese world truly everyone knows us, as, despite the enormous distances involved, the exchange of opinions between the various cities is far more intensive than, say, between Hamburg and Lübeck.

The Yan-Huan Art Museum in Beijing

In addition to the differences of language and culture between Europeans and Chinese there are, naturally, also great differences as regards the mentality and the manner of communication and cooperation. We as western Europeans and particularly as Germans must learn to be patient in all our activities in China and not to insist on rapid decisions in an excessively goal-oriented way. We have learnt that a polite Chinese person never says an absolute "no" and we have come to understand that at times the word "perhaps" can mean much the same as no. Used as we are to stating our opinion in a very direct manner without beating around the bush, the constant reference to the fact that losing face is a major disgrace for the Chinese and that therefore every effort must be made to avoid this is something that has to be kept in mind.

What I find particularly pleasant is the ritualized approach to life. Not everything happens in one go, people take their time. Consequently we have learnt to appreciate the fact that business meetings and contract negotiations are regularly accompanied by social activities such as taking a meal together and exchanging toasts, which makes the time spent together and the exchange of opinions all the more pleasant. Conversations are also conducted in metaphors. A metaphorical discussion is conducted at a very relaxed level and is, in a certain sense, ambiguous. However it is difficult for us to understand and to master the sophisticated tactics used in negotiation. We repeatedly have the feeling that we are inferior in this area.

We have also had to learn that political labels can mean very different things. Many activities and types of behavior in China are more capitalistic and oriented towards making money and profit than here in the West. Even if one ignores for the moment the language barrier, working together with Chinese architects, authorities and building contractors results in different impressions. On the one hand this collaboration can be friendly, positive and dynamic, but on the other hand it is also frequently characterized by misunderstandings, occasional distrust and differences of understanding. In working with private clients we have noticed that, to a far greater extent than is the case in Germany and Europe, clients like to use us as foreign architects to push through the utilization of a site – that is the client's interest in the profitable implementation of his project – against the interests of the city. Time and time again private clients expect us to plan more building mass and volume on a site than is officially allowed, in the hope that our name can help to secure permission for this additional exploitation of the site. But these attempts are not always successful and have meant above all that many of our projects have to be reworked a number of times until they finally represent a compromise between client, architect and city.

Dinner with business associates

I am impressed by the dynamism, the speed and, in a certain sense, the openness to the new, the eagerness to try out and implement new things – and all of this linked to speedy decision-making processes. What in Germany proceeds at a snail's pace happens in China at breathtaking speed. For example one of our Chinese clients, the owner of one of China's largest travel agencies, made a decision about an investment of 70–80 million dollars by himself in the space of only two hours. This kind of thing is completely unimaginable in Germany. However many decisions are made arbitrarily, that is to say they are not necessarily based on experience but rather on gut feeling.

Chinese (non)urbanity
"My evaluation of Chinese architecture, Chinese architects and Chinese building practice today "

Chinese skyline

My first impression of the cities and the landscape was one of uncontrolled growth and lack of structure. Cities had no center, no beginning, no end and no transition. I traveled by car from Shanghai to Nanjing, a distance of around 150 kilometers and despite careful attention I did not notice where Shanghai ended and Nanjing began. Whenever a suggestion of open landscape appeared one of the high-rise housing estates would loom into view. The urban sprawl is without any recognizable conceptual structure or an urban hierarchy, everything happens according to the principle of fortuity.

But the Chinese themselves also regard this uncontrolled growth as something negative; they notice the lack of contrasts. The fact that today pseudo-idyllic estates with an Italian or Spanish stamp are being created everywhere, small Disneylands with parks and areas of water, illustrates the need for identification, for a certain form of expression, for something that is unmistakably one's own.

More recently major efforts to eliminate deficits in this area have become evident. For example the discussion on traditional architecture and historic building methods in China is at least as developed as in Europe but with one important difference. In terms of their size, the number of floors they have and their structural order, European historic buildings, which in some cases are re-erected as replicas – for example the Royal Palace in Berlin with its Baroque façades and a new form of building in the interior – are almost always of a size and form that allows present-day requirements to be accommodated in them.

In contrast, in China buildings with floor areas of 50,000, 100,000, 150,000 or even 250,000 square meters are erected as a single building. This immense jump in scale has absolutely nothing in common with the traditional small-scale architecture of China, which is why traditional attributes applied as decoration to a façade, or motifs traced in mirror glass building fronts tend to look like a caricature.

On the other hand it is also important to say that a large number of the Chinese who make up the growth in the urban population come from the countryside, from small villages where, however quaint or picturesque they may look from a Western point of view, people live in unhygienic and anti-social conditions. When these people come to a major city the aesthetic chaos is of very little importance to them, compared with the gain in comfort. They no longer have to walk kilometers by foot, but can hop on a bus; they have running, indeed hot water, or an air conditioning unit on the façade – these represent major advances. The population pressure in the cities is enormous; wages in the city are almost three times higher than those in the countryside. Most of the buildings sites, including ours, rely up to 80 per cent on what are known as itinerant workers who are told only on site what they have to do, say to turn a concrete mixer or to carry stones or bore a hole. They work from twelve to sixteen hours a day, sleep on the building site in the simplest of sheds, and cook their rice soup on small stoves. And with the money they earn they can feed a large family at home that cannot earn anything like the same amount from agriculture. During the harvest they travel home for several weeks and then return to the building site. These building workers are unbelievably frugal and absolutely without emotions. If you tell someone in the evening that he should tear down the wall he has built during the day, he starts to do this immediately, without grumbling. There is no sense of identification with the work.

Chinese building site

Changes that took place in Europe in the course of two centuries in China take only a fraction of this time. On this account one can predict that the situation, currently regarded by investors as almost paradisiacal, can only remain as it is for a limited time. And incidentally, my impression is that the demand for intellectual and creative achievements is always primarily a need to learn. Behind it is the wish to take a look at everything, to copy it and to make it oneself the next time. The Chinese learn extremely fast. And therefore I am convinced that they are going to build more than just the Transrapid maglev train themselves. The refusal of our branch in Europe to do something that others have already done is an attitude completely foreign to the Chinese.

We are frequently confronted with a situation where a Chinese client believes that by acquiring our preliminary design he has purchased a successful and easily marketable idea and that he can from this point on, using his own means to a certain extent, cobble together everything on the spot. Naturally in terms of quality little survives of the original overall aim. Much is lost and is far too easily and quickly sacrificed and changed. A multitude of compromises are made, above all unsatisfactory ones, at a considerable cost to the quality of the architecture. The end result is that a well worked out concept is given an unsuccessful, bastardized form.

Clients believe that by not continuing to employ us after we have delivered the preliminary design they can save themselves money and can better implement their own decisions with the help of submissive and obedient offices. For example, a client for whom we designed an enormous complex with four high-rise buildings showed us to the door because an office in Hong Kong promised to do the job for him far more inexpensively. There were no discussions about copyright. Their approach was that they had paid us for the paper and the travel costs and were even willing to mount our name on the completed building! They could not understand that this was not what we wanted. Only in the end do they discover that they do not receive the quality product they had originally wished for.

We see ourselves as responsible for the architecture product in its entirety and therefore in such a situation, if a client implements one of our designs only more or less as we planned it (and it is generally less rather than more), we can only accept this after putting up considerable resistance and at the cost of our true goals.

This is particularly true in the field of housing. In China at present public housing subsidized by state funds is as good as non-existent. Housing is commercial and is erected by the private economy. Dwellings can be sold at considerable profit, which in turn heats up the building boom. However these apartments are in a condition that would never be accepted in Germany. They frequently have no flooring, no doors, no washbasins, and no toilet bowl or bathtub. As this is the only kind of apartment that most of the Chinese can afford they move into the dwelling in this incomplete state and camp out there for years. There is a water supply pipe and a waste pipe, then a bucket is brought along, this is also used as a toilet, an open fire is made on the floor screed, people sit on low mattresses. In China there will soon be an unbelievable collection of building defects, as many of the buildings there that have been hastily cobbled together will not have a long life. But, as our specific goal is to carry out high quality architecture in a comprehensive sense, we wish for a change of attitude in this regard on the part of our Chinese clients and commissioners.

What I most regret is the fact that among the many new buildings erected in recent years in China there are hardly any noticeable differences between the work of Chinese architects and that of foreigners. They all apparently have in common: the imitation of American models, the use of materials that symbolize high-tech and progress and the combination of these with supposedly traditional Chinese elements as decoration.

While searching for an original Chinese architecture I spent an entire day in a bookshop in Shanghai and bought everything they had about architecture in this city. And I found out that there are some things that look like Miami, others like Cuba, then there is Belle Epoque and Art Déco and Art Nouveau, there is a British Quarter, a French Quarter, an Italian Quarter, a German Quarter. Where are the Chinese roots to be found here?

As I mentioned at the outset, for me in almost all Chinese cities there is no recognizable hierarchical and structural strategy. In my opinion decisions are far too often fragmented, that is to say they are made in terms of individual projects while neglecting the overall urban context. As a result much of the specific identity of individual Chinese towns is being lost. If one compares the traditional differences between the lifestyles and demands on the urban structures and living environment in Europe and in China one soon sees that these differences are enormous. By now the development of China is approaching at a dynamic pace the structural characteristics of American cities with the dominant role being played by motorized traffic. In contrast in the majority of European cities the traditional character and the typical aspects of the city have been preserved down to the present day. One can identify cities such as Paris, London, Berlin or Milan with one's nose. Just the smell, the atmosphere alone of the respective city is enough to identify it. This applies to many urban districts and spaces, not only to landmarks or the major buildings visited by tourists.

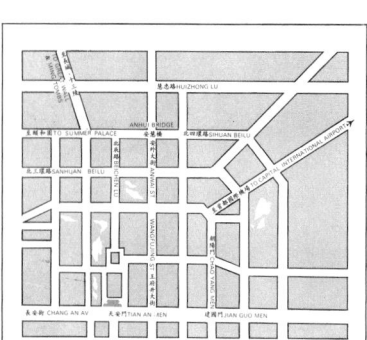

Ring structure of Beijing

As a result of this it has by and large proved possible to preserve identity in urban planning in Europe. In China in contrast the impact of modernization means that almost everything that traditionally shaped the character – apart from a few important buildings and monuments – has been destroyed and replaced by new buildings and in the process the streets have assumed enormous widths. A complete change of scale has taken place that has given almost all cities the same characteristics. Although today one can still recognize the ring structure of Peking with the low center of the Forbidden City as a structural characteristic, and the dominance of the many elevated roads is clearly evident in Guangzhou, as is the duality of Bund and Shanghai-Pudong along the Yangtze river, as soon as one leaves the striking centers of the cities the image blurs to form a diffuse monotony without identity or characteristics.

The architectural development of recent years has led to the loss of part of the country's identity, while the imitation of American models demonstrates a kind of pseudo-progressiveness that is often combined in a most superficial way with stylistic elements à la chinoise. Only in rare cases is the most recent architecture in any way experimental; generally it consists of façade-shows that have little relationship to the function or use of the building. This architecture may be striking, it may advertise itself, but like at a big carnival where everyone is dressed in as striking a costume as possible, the individual impact is lost in the sum of those striving to make an impression.

Façade detail

The only thing that will have any lasting quality is an architecture that is generated from the conditions, from the social context, from the function, from consideration of the urban context, from the economy and, ultimately, from a timeless design intent.

One theme that I am regularly confronted with – against the background of the CO_2 debate currently being conducted in Europe – is that of ecology and sustainability. From the start of my activities in China I have been surprised by the minor role played in new buildings in China by the use of energy. In hot regions glass buildings are erected without any external sunscreens, which means that they require a substantial amount of energy for cooling purposes. Even in Peking, which has a lengthy cold season during the year, the windows in offices and apartments have only single glazing, which results in high energy use to heat spaces.

For me the question of sustainability and durability is also a question of mental constancy or steadfastness. Buildings that indulge in fashion of one kind or another, in which the use and function do not correspond with the design and form, which are just superficially decorated, which use transient materials such as mirror glass and other flashy building materials are, like fashionable items of clothing, short-lived. As regards the durability of materials there is also need for a commitment to natural materials, which invariably have a longer life than artificial building materials. The former include steel and glass, aluminum and wood, just as much as bricks and the traditional materials of the respective country.

But the question of how energy is used, of performance in the respective climatic zone is also of major importance for permanence and sustainability. On this account when we design buildings for subtropical zones in China we use adjustable screen elements (which is something new there) to provide shade in front of the façades in order on the one hand to save energy and on the other to improve the usability of the interior, no matter whether the building contains offices or apartments.

Transformed architecture
"Why, what and how I design for China"

I am often asked what models I use in China to establish a relationship to a particular site. I think this is the wrong question. What Chinese society produces today has absolutely nothing to do with the Chinese tradition and with earlier social customs, including those to do with hygiene. Occasionally it is pointed out to us that the Royal Palace in Berlin is going to be reconstructed and that therefore it should be possible to do the same with Chinese models. But there is a decisive difference here. As already mentioned, due to the size, the number of floor levels or the depth of historic European buildings it is very much feasible to accommodate modern functions in them – such as libraries, museums or administration offices. In contrast the traditional Chinese way of building – apart from the grand formal buildings – was at such a small scale, generally single-story, that it is completely unsuitable for the demands of present-day uses. In addition there is also the fact that building projects in China today are generally far larger than those we are familiar with. And then all that remains is the pagoda roof on the 50th floor as a decorative "cocktail cherry" justified by tradition or in terms of spiritual references.

Continuity can be best achieved by transforming certain phenomena of Chinese history and way of life.

One tradition of the Chinese way of life was integration within the system of the extended family. This was reflected in typologies such as the courtyard house in which individual buildings were combined to form an ensemble that related to a courtyard. The buildings were always single-story. Hygiene services such as water pumps or latrines were communal facilities. This aspect was completely ignored by socialist building methods, in which units were simply stacked without any consideration of family connections – and this approach was accompanied by the single-child family planning policy.

When in our urban planning projects today we speak of traditional structures we are not referring to the same scale but to a transformation. We form districts, we create units of reasonable dimensions that are not anonymously absorbed in the urban structure.

I wish to introduce our design for Lingang New City as an example of this.

A decorated high-rise building façade

Lingang New City
The concept for Lingang New City is on the one hand indebted to the traditional European city, which, over the centuries, regularly developed out of space and urbanity: streets, squares, parks, promenades form the urban environment. But this concept is also revolutionary, it has something that no city has: at the center there is the vacuum of a lake with a diameter of 2.9 kilometers. There are a number of reasons for this. The center of the city is always the most desirable and expensive location. As banks, insurance companies and large businesses are better able to

afford expensive sites than the citizens for their residential districts this center is generally occupied by buildings representing the world of finance and on this account produces little in terms of urban quality.

Model of Lingang New City

Additionally the center is always subject to heavy traffic making it unattractive to average citizens, pedestrians and cyclists. The lake at the center of Lingang creates a communal leisure zone for sailing and swimming, presents public buildings on its artificial islands and on the periphery offers a promenade nine kilometers long which has far more "first addresses" than the concentrated city.

Starting from the center the ring-shaped urban structures are articulated by means of a business district into a recreation zone laid out as a park ring with public buildings, and, on the periphery, into separate residential districts each with its own identity and individuality. The analogous structure of the city – similar to that of a compass or a watch – creates a clear orientation as one can always relate to the center of the lake that will be marked by a "cloud needle". This will mean that from every point within the city everyone will be able to find their way. On the other hand the radial articulation in sectors allows growth that follows the path taken by the hand of a watch. In the way it is generated this urban form reveals the sense and the rational analysis of well-functioning urban development. Secondary functions such as motorized traffic and public transport are integrated in this system in such a way that they serve urban life rather than hindering it.

In Lingang there are 13 large districts each with 18,000 inhabitants and each with its own center; at the next scale there are smaller units with communal public areas grouped around courtyard structures. Here children can play, people can meet at the "washing square", smoke a pipe or play dominos.

The buildings are five to six stories high with courtyards measuring 30 by 30 meters. Whether extended families living in a kind of spatial connection still exist – apart from in the country – I tend to doubt. But city apartments with three or four rooms are often occupied by twelve people. This suggests that several generations live under one roof.

From the very outset Lingang was conceived to meet the highest social aspirations and for this reason will be carried out by partners from Europe and the USA, as well as Chinese investors. Lingang New City, designed for a total of 800,000 inhabitants, is to be the gateway to China, a free-trade zone with the most highly qualified production places and technology firms. The standard of fitting-out will approximately match European standards.

I should like below to deal with a number of questions, which are among those I am most often asked about Lingang.

1. Can Lingang become a functioning city?
2. What do you orient yourself on when designing the façades, forms and materials so that in the end Lingang will look like China rather than Poppenbüttel (i.e. a district of Hamburg, Germany)?
3. Can a city such as Lingang really be built from scratch? Should a city not be a naturally growing formation?
4. Is Lingang a utopian city?

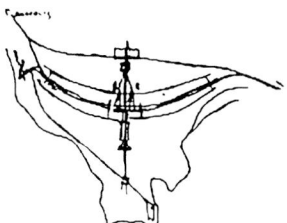

To 1: From my position it is somewhat difficult to answer this question. Instead of an expensive city center Lingang will have an attractive ring. And there is a further problem that affects the city. The master plan is one thing, implementing it is another. And there are disagreements at this interface. At variance with the intentions of the master plan the streets are getting wider and wider, making it more difficult to create urbanity. On the other hand what I see are negative accompanying factors make clear that an emerging city is subject to a process of development. Both the architect and the future residents must live with the momentary records of this process.

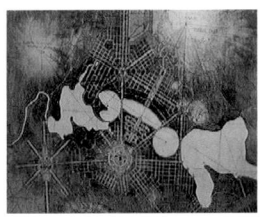

To 2: Interestingly, in the Shanghai region widespread use is made of a dark fired brick that we also know in Hamburg and therefore I have no reservations about using it there, even though many average Chinese citizens regard it as the cheapest of materials and would far rather have mirror glass. And it is the customer who pays.

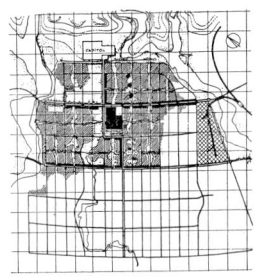

To 3: To corroborate this question unsuccessful examples of urban planning such as Brasilia or the Indian city Chandigarh are frequently cited. Every artificial formation that is developed in a single holistic process is, naturally, exposed to the danger of failure. But this can be kept under control. As far as Brasilia or Chandigarh or also Canberra are concerned, in my estimation none of these examples, is, for a number of reasons, a good city. For example, Brasilia was founded on the glorification of mobility. The car and freedom of movement were seen as highly important and all other functions were made subordinate to them – this is still the basic characteristic of every American city.

In contrast to these historic examples Lingang is not based on technical mobility but on the human scale. I believe that the urban structure of Lingang offers a good basis for urbanity but above all Lingang avoids one thing: the creation of a city center occupied by buildings. Instead of a dense center there is a nine-kilometer-long lakeshore band and as a result it is possible to give a very large number of buildings the first address in the city. With a view of the lake – what could be better?

Concept sketches of Brasilia, Canberra, Chandigarh

To 4: No, at the very latest when it is built Lingang will no longer be a utopian city. But there is something that almost borders on a utopia: first the sea was filled in to create land for the city then the center was excavated once again. The characteristics of this process, which is itself difficult to grasp, may possibly have a utopian quality. But I am convinced that China urgently needs such utopian concepts. I never thought that we would win the competition with this initially (and I emphasize the word initially) utopian project for Lingang. Here a utopia has become reality.

View ahead
"The aspects of Chinese architecture that I regard as needing reform"

In my opinion China, on account of its history, its dynamic growth and the leap into modernity, should commit itself to an independent culture that does not copy, uses no clichés and neither denies the quantum leap in dimensions nor seeks to embellish it. The decisions on urban planning structures should be made strictly and exclusively according to conceptual criteria and individual economic interests should be ordered within a clear hierarchy.

The architecture that is generally preferred today with its pseudo-historic trimmings and decorative, superficial Chinese ingredients derived from superstition is suitable only for creating facelessness. Only a courageous contemporary architecture can leave impressive traces behind it.

One cannot disguise a 60-story skyscraper as a doll's house. But one can find a new form of expression for it that derives character and quality from the building's use, its size, and its construction.

The question as to how I believe an "architecture with Chinese characteristics" should look calls to my mind the German fairy tale "Little Red Riding Hood and the Wolf": in the story the wolf disguises himself as the innocuous grandmother so that he can capture and devour the little girl (Red Riding Hood). For many people (not only in China) modern-day architecture is like the wolf: the attempt to make it look friendly and sweet like a grandmother has failed, and time and time again such attempts end unsuccessfully. Taming the wolf and deriving a positive expression of his character from his own qualities is the real task that needs to be tackled.

Reasonably enough after all these critical remarks I am asked what I would do differently. I believe that there are many areas in need of reform, not just in China but also here in Germany. Throughout Asia, including Japan, I note a lack of coordinated urban planning that understands urban space in its entirety and exerts a regulating effect on architecture. I believe it is necessary that urban space, that is to say streets, squares, and parks, should gain a greater importance for urban quality, and that architecture, the element that defines and borders space, should be used as a means of achieving this goal.

But today it is generally the case that the separate exploitation of every single site allows the development of a heterogeneous system without any context. The result is that no clearly defined street spaces are created nor does there exist any kind of homogeneity in the style of architecture or the height of the buildings.

It seems to me that the quality of detailing in Chinese architecture is also in need of reform. Many buildings are put together hastily and at great speed without the details being carefully planned in advance by the architect. This not only impairs the buildings' aesthetic value but, likewise, also negatively affects their suitability for use and above all the lifespan of architecture.

Despite all these critical observations I nevertheless want to emphasize that for me personally conceiving projects in China is a source of great joy, as I have the feeling, far more than in Germany and Europe, that in terms of ideas and thoughts I am able to draw on a great wealth of resources. One is given the chance to present a strong idea conceptually without the fear that one may have infringed on a lot of restrictions and regulations.

And it is a particular source of satisfaction that our projects, with which we compete in many places in China against colleagues from the USA, Japan and naturally China as well meet with acceptance and recognition, although or perhaps precisely because our architecture is so clearly and strongly different from that of our colleagues.

In this book we document for the first time projects that were carried out in the years 1998 to 2008. Many projects are still at the construction or planning stage and in the near future the chapter on "gmp in China" will certainly continue.

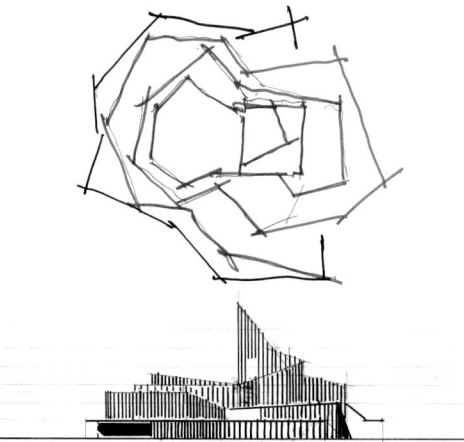

Sketch of the Performance Art Center

Kelamayi

Turugart
Pass
3752

Akesu
Kuche
Bohu
(Bagrax)
Ku'erle
Turpan
(Tulufan)
Qijiaojing
Yandun

Kashi

Bo Hu

Pamir

Shache
Talimu Pendi
XINJIANG

Lop Nor
(Luobu Po)

Shule He

Eji'naqi

Anxi
Dunhuang
Jiayuguan
Badain
Jaran

Yecheng
Takla Makan
(Takelamagan Shamo)

Kumutage Shamo

Yumen
Zhangye

Mazatage Feng
1570 m
Hetian
Ruoqiang
Qiemo
A'erjin Shan
Mangnai
Chaidamu
Pendi

Qilian Shan
Nan Shan
Jinchang
Wu

Mazar

Qiaogeli Feng
(K2) 8611 m

Yutian
Minfeng

Kunlun Shan
Muzitage Feng
7723 m
6860 m

Delingha
Tianjun

Qing
Hai

Ge'ermu
(Golmud)
QINGHAI
Gonghe
Xinin

Qing-Zang Gaoyuan

Zhaling
Hu
Huangheyan
Huang He

Shiquanhe

TIBET
(XIZANG)
Geladandong Feng
6621 m

Bayankala Shan
Darlag

Gartok
Kailash 6714 m
Darchen

Lagu
Tanggula-
Pass
5230
5500 m

Himalaya (Ximalaya Shan)

Seling
Tso
Amdo
Yushu

Tangra
Yumco
Naqu
Sog
Nangqian
Dege
Aba

Pazagug

Luhuo
Dadu He

Chamdo
Bamda

INDIA
NEPAL
Lhatse Dzong
Lhasa
Gyimda
Medu Gongkar

Jangtsekiang
Batang
Kangding

SICHUAN
Ya

Tschomolangma
(Mt. Everest) 8848 m
Shigatse
Yarlung Tsangpo (Bramaputra

Nu Jiang

BHUTAN
Kagebo
6740
Deqin
Xichang
Zhongdian

Lancang Jiang
Lijiang

Dali
Er Hai
Dongchua
Kunmi

Xiaguan
Dian Chi

Luxi
Fengqing
Ye

Ruili
Lincang
YUNNAN

MYANMAR
(BURMA)
Mekong
Gejiu

Pu'er

Jinghong
Mengla

THAILAND
LAOS

THE LINGANG PROJECT

LINGANG NEW CITY, NEAR SHANGHAI
上海临港新城

Competition 2002 – 1st prize
Design Meinhard von Gerkan
Partner Nikolaus Goetze
Design team Jessica Weber, Annika Schröder, Beate Quaschning, Christoph Böttinger, Wei Wu, Sigrid Müller, Eduard Kaiser, Hung-Wei Hsu, Richard Sprenger, Stephanie Heß, Christian Krüger, Hector Labin, Markus Carlsen
Port planning HPC Hamburg Port Consulting
Landscape architects Breimann & Bruun
Light planning Schlotfeldt Licht
Client Shanghai Harbour City Development (Group) Co., Ltd.
Mr. Bao Tieming
Area 74,000 m²
Inhabitants 800,000 (in 2020)
Construction period 2003–2020

01 The new city,
60 km away from Shanghai
02 Lingang New City with
satellites and industry zone

Opposite page
Master plan of
Lingang New City by
Meinhard von Gerkan

Following page
Model view of the concept
at night

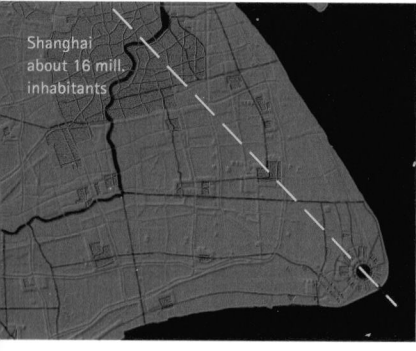

01

02

Shanghai

Shanghai is both a significant commercial center and at the same time a traffic junction within China. There are plans to develop Shanghai, a historically and culturally important city, into an international commercial, financial and trade metropolis in the future. The rapidly increasing population of Shanghai, today nearly 13 million, will reach 16 million by 2020, 13.6 million of which will live in the city. Shanghai's city center will then have an estimated surface area of 600,000 m² and approximately 8 million inhabitants. In order to accommodate the huge growth of population and industry in Shanghai, the city-planning department conducted an international competition for the planning of a new harbor city that incorporates the international deep-sea container harbor Yangshan. The first prize of the competition, which took place in several stages, was awarded to the Hamburg architecture office gmp. The newly-planned satellite city Lingang New City is intended to provide space for 800,000 inhabitants in an area of 74,000 m² and represents, alongside Chandigarh, Brasilia and Canberra, the only city of this scale to be founded in the past hundred years.

Urban Planning Concept

The concept for Lingang New City takes up the ideals of the traditional European city and combines it with a "revolutionary" idea: instead of a high-density center, the focal point will be a circular lake with a diameter of 2.9 km and a 9-km lakeside promenade with a bathing beach à la Copacabana in the heart of the city. Cultural buildings and leisure facilities are located on islands, which can be accessed by boat. The design was inspired by the city of Alexandria, one of the Seven Wonders of the World; the quality of life provided by the close proximity to water draws its references from Hamburg. The whole city structure is based on the metaphor of an image of concentric ripples, formed by a drop falling into water. In line with this allegory, the utility structures are ordered in the form of concentric rings spreading outwards from the central Dishui Lake: from the promenade, through to the extremely dense business district, a circular city park, 500 m in width, which incorporates solitary public buildings, to the block-like living quarters for 13,000 inhabitants respectively. The city ring between the lakeside promenade and the green belt, the business district, forms the center of city life. A mix of offices, shops, arcades, pedestrian precincts and dense living space is located here. The concentric structure is layered following the principle of a compass rose; the streets and pathways radiate out from the center. These provide the city with a clear, ordered structure and divide the built-up rings into separate sectors.

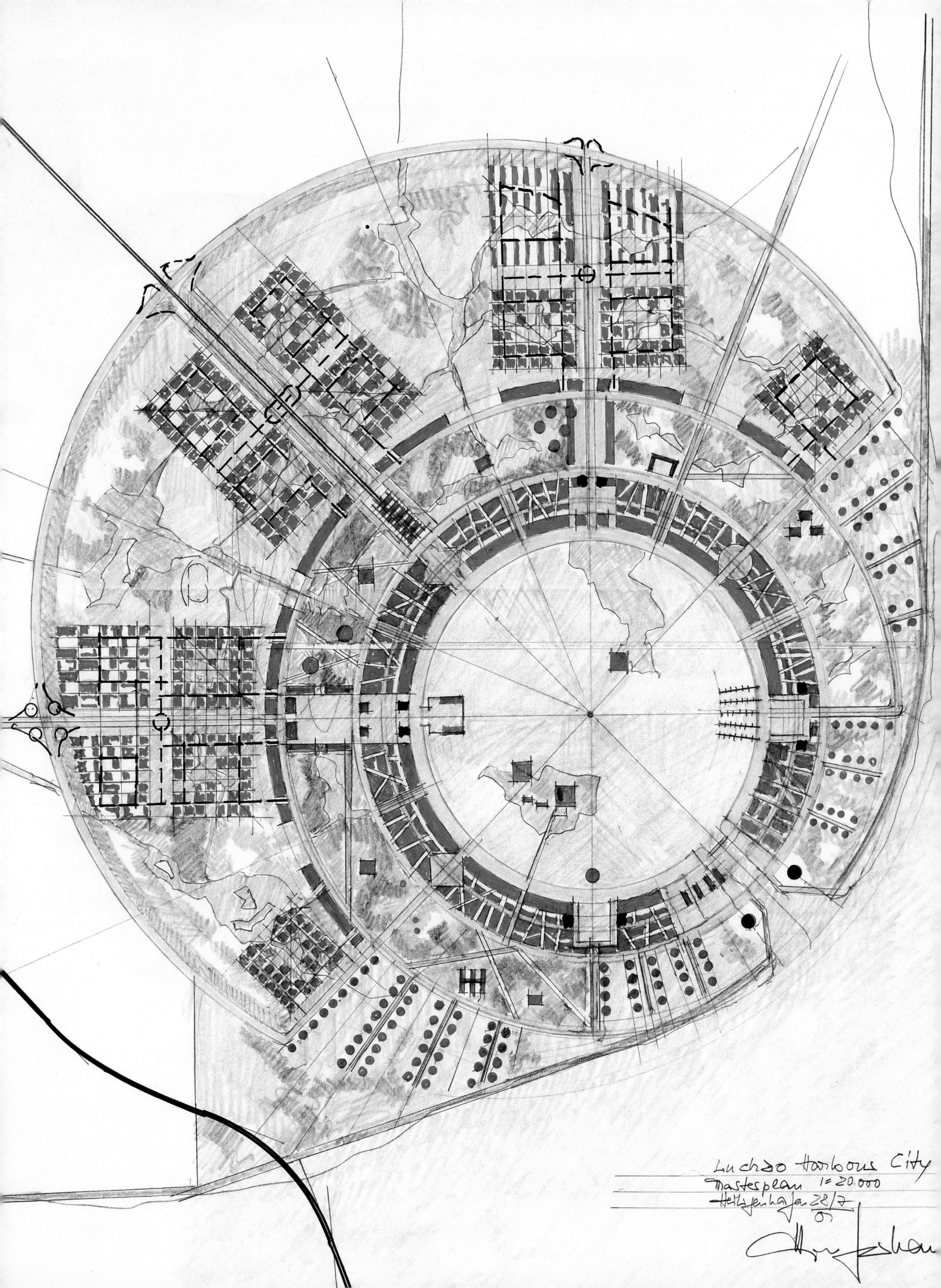

Luchao Harbour City
Masterplan 1=20.000
Hertzenhafen 28/7
05

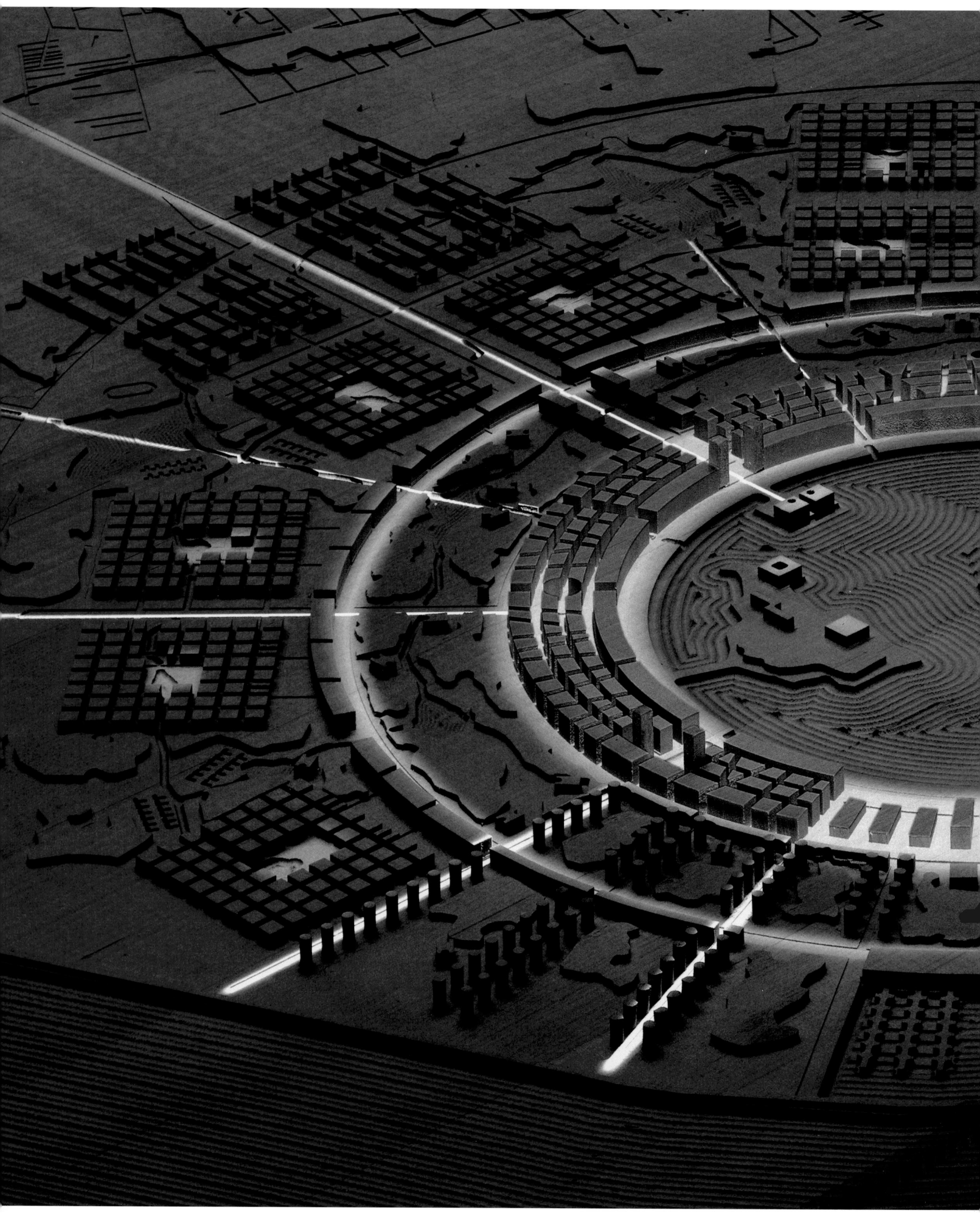

In this way, an ideal network of access is created within which the city can also expand above and beyond the planned scale. The countryside penetrates like wedges as far as the second ring. Waterways and small lakes extend into all quarters underlining the central theme of "waterside living" in a wide variety of forms. The public transport system with light trains at street level functions as a circular railway with adjoining loops.

Ring Development

All three layers of the ring development will be characterized by dense building blocks broken up by squares in each quarter and small pocket parks. The promenade ring provides a fantastic view across the lake whilst the next city ring is traffic-free and characterized by its shopping facilities. Finally, the adjacent park ring provides an attractive location between the city park and the lake. Its northern part can accommodate living quarters. Each of the three layers has its own characteristic face. Differentiation in the height of the blocks, the choice of building materials and the design of the exterior provides exciting diversity. At the same time they all fit a common city-planning canon and the individual buildings can be plausibly seen as part of the whole, forming an ensemble. In the selection of the building materials for the Lingang New City, it is important to consider the ancient building tradition of China, in particular in the Shanghai region. A successful mixture of cultural tradition

01 Satellite photo before the land reclamation
02 Satellite photo of the land reclamation for Lingang New City 2003 …
03 … and 2006

02   03

and modern European architectural styles will give Lingang an unmistakable identity. The 14 living quarters, grouped in the third ring around the center, are embedded as defined, identifiable areas in the expanded countryside area of the Nanhui province. These self-sustaining mini-centers with shops, services, basic medical care, kindergartens and crèches form self-sufficient communities. Whilst their common size, grid and basic module, as well as a predetermined canon of materials show that they are clearly part of a group, the design of the public spaces gives each of them a unique character. The squares and public parks are strongly influenced by international harbor cities which serve as models of inspiration, thus allowing scope for individuality and an unmistakable identity.

Radial Structure
The radial structure which divides the city rings into individual segments has squares of different shapes and sizes along its length. The most striking of the squares is the Main Square on the west-east axis. It serves as the prelude and invitation to a stroll along the lakeside promenade and an attraction for tourists from all over the world. The likewise radial city canals have an important function for the city water supply but equally serve to give structure and identity to the inner city area. Their individual design and profile give each canal its own character and identity.
The names of the canals are reminiscent of the great rivers of the world (Mississippi, Ganges, Volga, Yangtse etc.).

01 Open space that does not obtain a
rate of return upgrades those
areas adjoining the water, which is
omnipresent.

Opposite page
The "cloud needle" ascends from the
middle of the central lake as
Lingang New City's primary landmark.

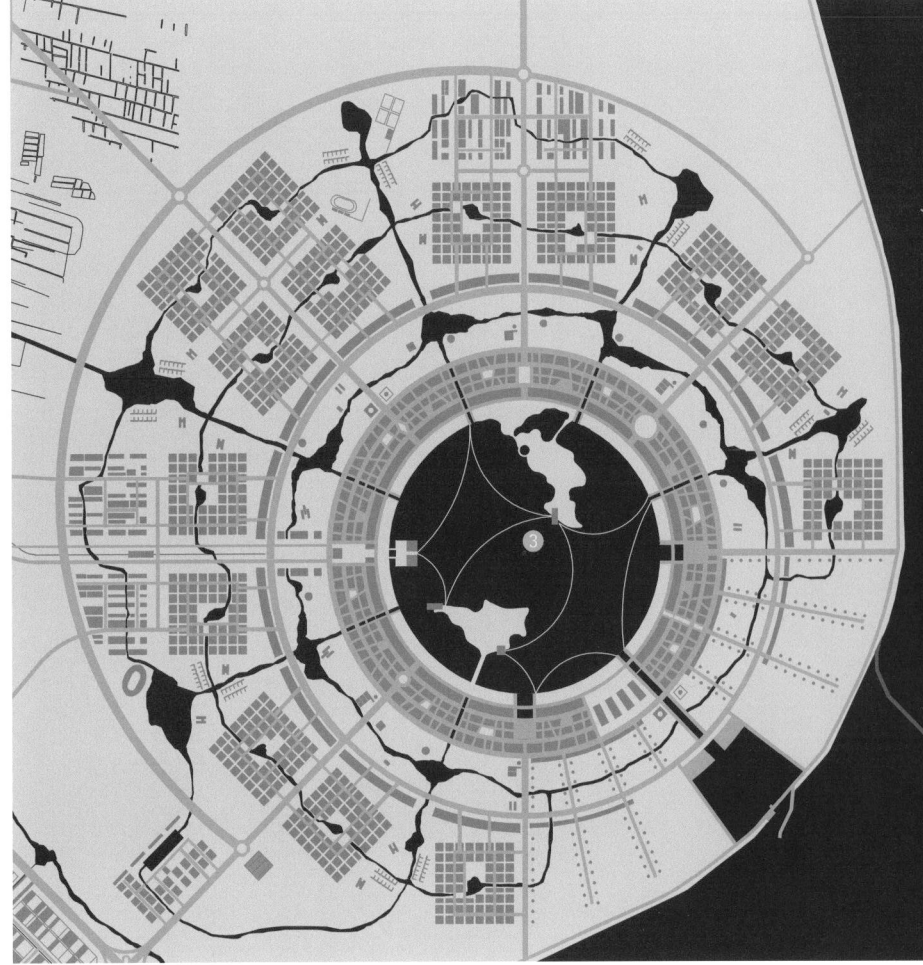

01

Landmarks

The landmarks are to a large extent visible representatives of the being and the
substance of Lingang. The economic source, origin and culture of the city are
manifested in them. They are solitary buildings, filigree and glass in their materiality.
Like glowing crystals they are allegories to the urban community and thus provide
the city center with an architectural identity.

Realization

The first construction phase of the new city for 80,000 inhabitants in the present
mainland area should be completed by 2008. The second and third phases of
construction will follow until 2020. The area required for this was dragged up from
the ocean by means of an earth bank. In the process of obtaining this land, the
Dishui Lake was formed as the central point of the new harbor city.
At present gmp are planning amongst others the "cloud needle", the first segment of
the so-called New Bund and Western Island. The Maritime Museum and the opposite
Shanghai Nanhui District Administration Center are to be completed in 2008.

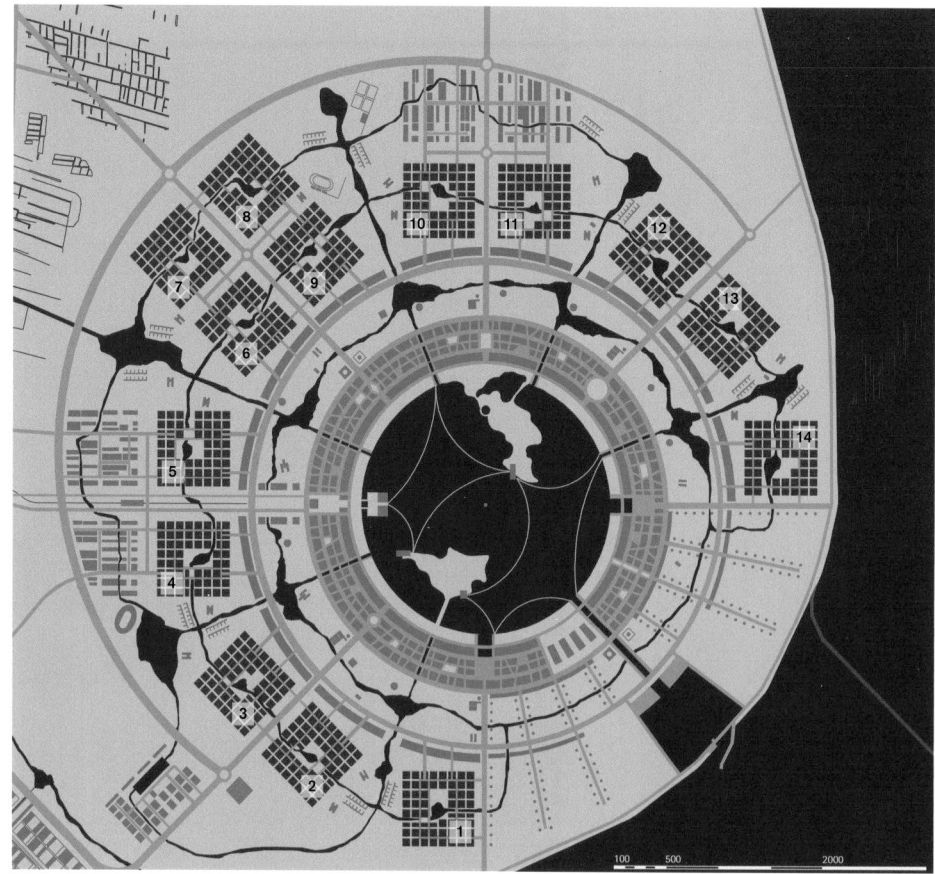

01

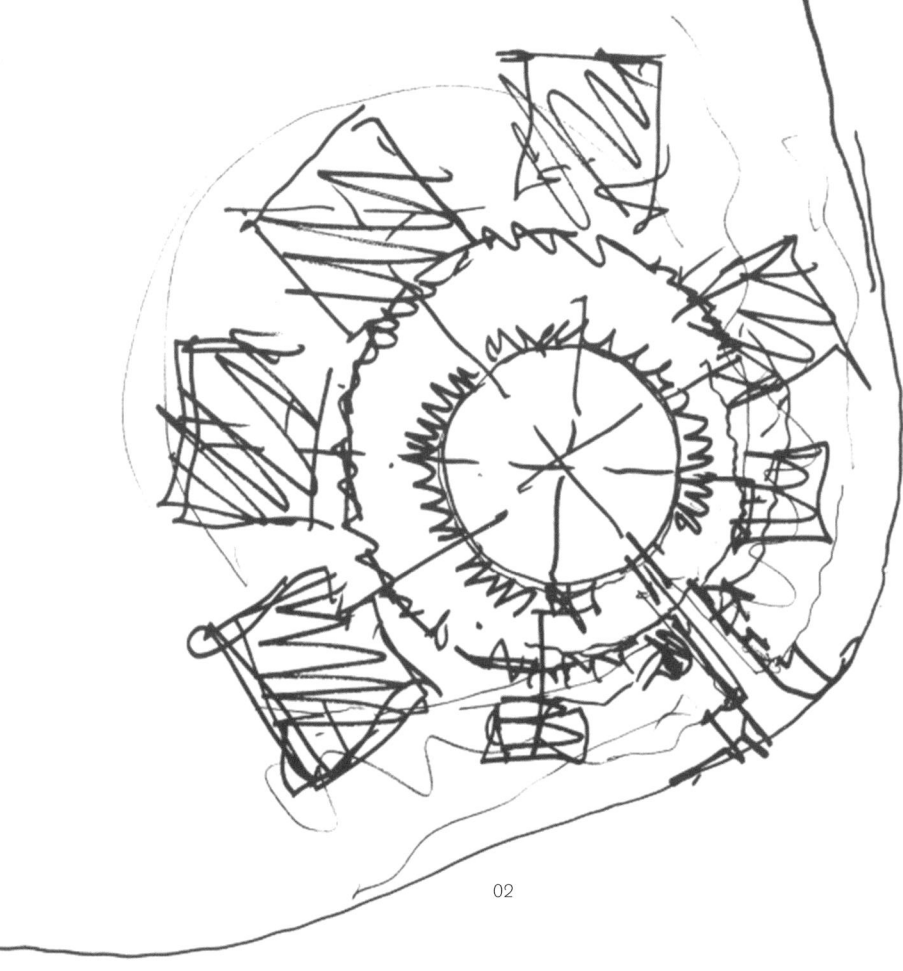

02

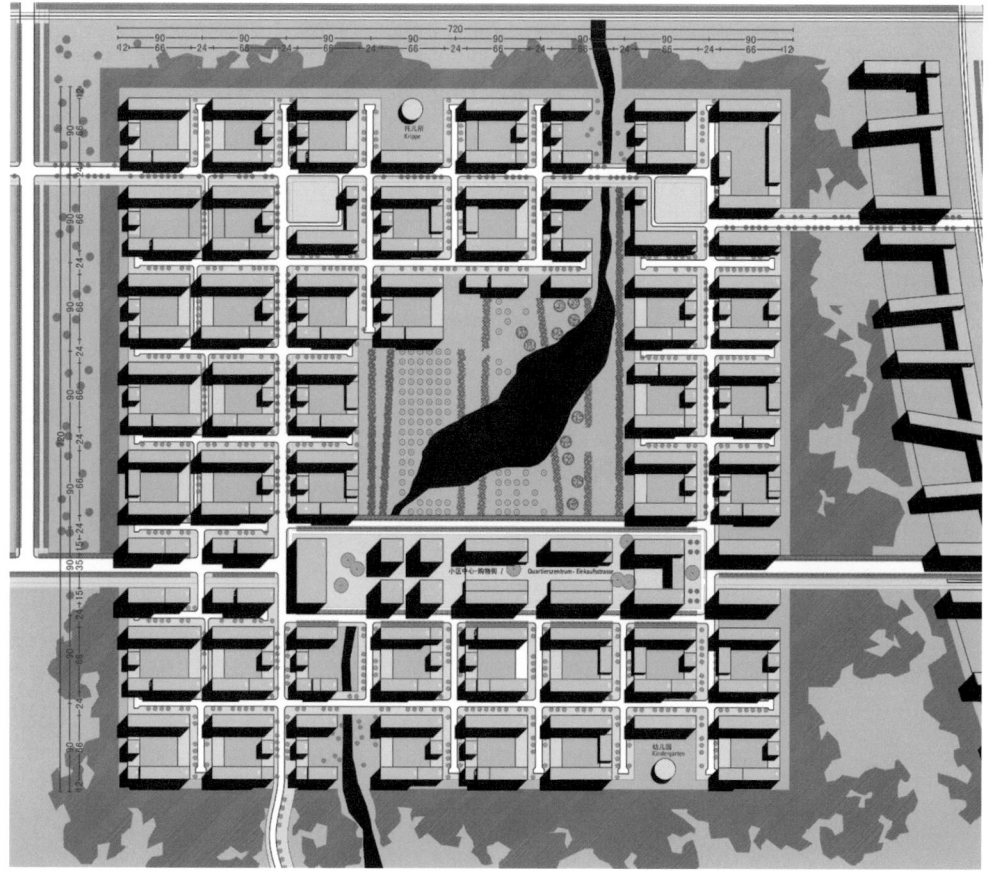

03

02 Sketch by Meinhard von Gerkan
03 The "Hamburg Quarter" is one
   of the 14 residential quarters for
   13,000 inhabitants.
04 Rendering of a housing impression

04

31

01

02

03

04

Housing variants in the
"Hamburg Quarter"
01 Charles de Picciotto
02 Anja Meding
03 Walter Gebhardt
04 Philipp Kamps
05 Michael Biwer
06 Johann von Mansberg

THE "HAMBURG QUARTER", LINGANG NEW CITY

临港新城汉堡小区

Designs by Michael Biwer, Walter Gebhardt, Philipp Kamps,
Johann von Mansberg, Anja Meding, Charles de Picciotto

"hamburg architects" is an association of these six architects. All of
them were students of Meinhard von Gerkan and former employees
of his office "von Gerkan, Marg und Partner". The declared belief in
urban quality of life in the meeting of European and Chinese town
tradition is the most promising strategy of successful development of
living real estate in China. This is already carried out in examples on
the spot point.

ARCHETYPE BUILDING BLOCK AT THE NEW BUND, LINGANG NEW CITY

临港新城湖滨建筑典型设计

Consultancy 2005–2007
Design Meinhard von Gerkan
Design team Evelyn Pasdzierny, Alexandra Kühne
Client Shanghai Harbour City Investment Co.
Gross floor area 80,000 m²

The Archetype Building Block – like all buildings in the first ring – will incorporate a business zone on the ground floor that is accompanied by arcades. This enables a pleasant, protected walkway alongside the buildings both in summer and also on rainy days.

The façades facing the Dishui Lake have as a conception a play which emphasizes the vertical and horizontal lines. A staggered roof silhouette as well as plastic projections and recesses in the façades create lively differentiations, stage a diversified, dramaturgical play with light and shade. Façades made of light-colored natural stone evoke a bright and friendly atmosphere.

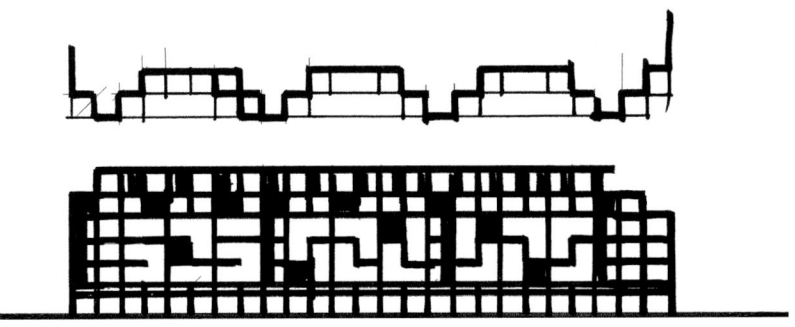

01

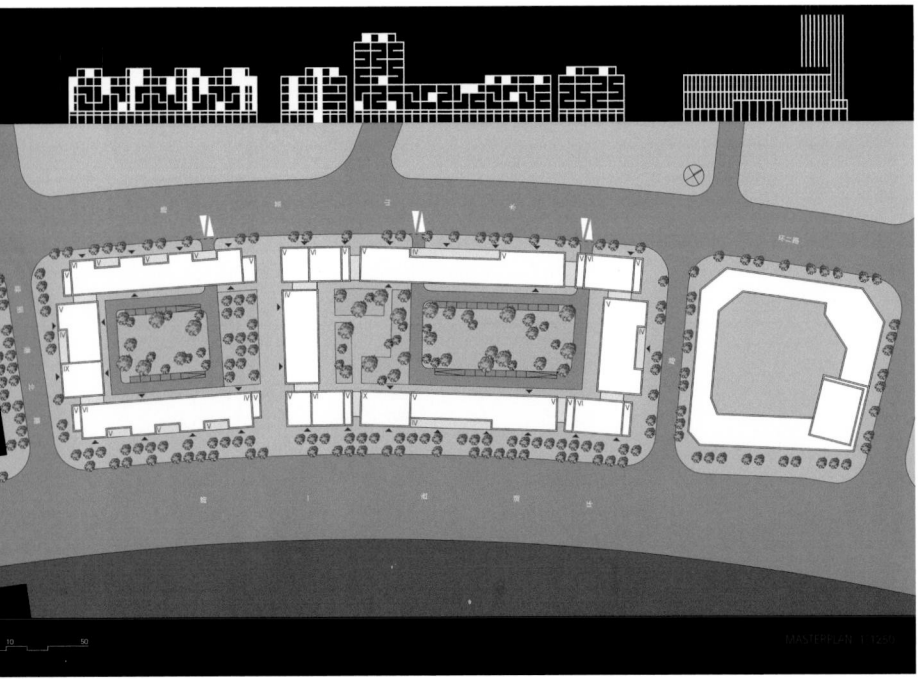

02

34

03

BUILDINGS AND PROJECTS

GERMAN SCHOOL AND APARTMENT HOUSE, BEIJING

北京德国使馆学校

Competition 1998 – 1st prize
Design Meinhard von Gerkan with Michael Biwer
Partner Klaus Staratzke
Project managers Michael Biwer, Sibylle Kramer
Design team Bettina Groß, Elke Hoffmeister
Project team Michèle Watenphul, Knut Maass, Ulrich Rösler,
Diana Heinrich, Jörn Bohlmann, Rüdiger von Helmolt, Robert Wildegger
Structural engineers Weber-Poll Ingenieure
Operating construction company Philipp Holzmann
Client Fed. Rep. of Germany
Gross floor area School 9,658 m², Apartment House 9,657 m²
Construction period 1999–2000

Due to the heterogeneous neighborhood the concept of a self-orientated building
complex was developed. The ensemble is formed by a horizontally emphasized
school building and a contrasting vertical residential complex. In the school building,
two three-storied building bars flank the central layer with special uses. An open
glass hall connects two parallel nine-storied building bars of the residential building.
The color concept of the imperial red and yellow colors in the school building is
repeated in the residential block. The school building with its red façade from
prefabricated concrete elements and red floorings in the interior is thus contrasted
with the residential block with its yellow prefabricated concrete façade elements as
well as yellow floorings.

01 Site plan
02 Section

Opposite page
The outdoor stairs serves
as an additional exit route.

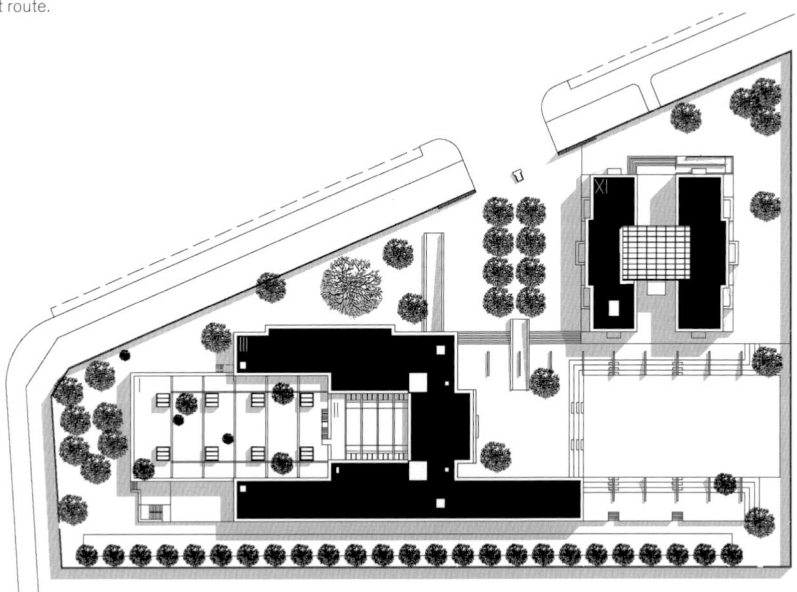

01

02

01

02

01 An outdoor sports field
is of high value in a densely
developed city.
02 View through the arcades,
following the open space
03 View onto the school roof
terrace. The vierendeel
girders span the sports hall
located underneath,
simultaneously serving as
spatial dividers.

INTERNATIONAL CONVENTION & EXHIBITION CENTER, NANNING

南宁国际会展中心

Competition 1999 – 1st prize
Design Meinhard von Gerkan and Nikolaus Goetze
Project managers Dirk Heller, Karen Schroeder
Design team Oliver Christ, Andreas Gärtner, Mike Berrier, Jens Niemann,
Antonio Caetita-Soeiro, Malte Wolf
Project team Christoph Berle, Kai Siebke, Georg Traun, Friedhelm Chlosta,
Meike Schmidt, Wencke Eissing, Oliver Christ, Stefanie Schupp,
Jochen Schwarz, Eckhard Send, Iris van Hülst, Thomas Eberhardt
Chinese partner practice Guangxi Architectural Comprehensive
Design & Research Institute
Client Nanning International Convention & Exhibition Co., Ltd.
Gross floor area 165,000 m²
Construction period 1999–2003/2005

01 Urban development model
02 Drawing by
Meinhard von Gerkan

Opposite page
Open-air terrace between
rotunda and exhibition halls

The site on a slope with a height difference of 45 m is located on the outskirts of Nanning within the green belt surrounding the city. A multifunctional hall with a folded domical roof, 70 m high and 48 m in diameter, forms the head of the exhibition complex and rises above the city silhouette as a landmark. The roof is conceived as a filigree load-bearing steel structure which is covered on both sides with a translucent membrane. Due to its central location the circular hall can be used separately from the exhibition and conference operations. Nine exhibition halls realized during the first construction phase all of them designed with two exhibition levels, can be interlinked on both levels as groups, providing for a variety of events. The dimension of the halls varies between 2,100 m² and 3,200 m², complemented by one hall with a floor area of 5,000 m². The halls are naturally lit on two sides and can be blacked out when required. A stone plinth forms the visual foundation; during events it can be used as an open-air terrace and exhibition area. Reinforced concrete columns positioned in front of the ascending stone socle stretch across the complete height of both hall levels and support the distinct roof which is rhythmically structured by the recesses of the cores accommodating the technical plant and services. Externally and internally stone, glass and concrete are the predominately used materials; colors were scarcely used and only applied for the accentuation of special functions. In 2005 the second construction phase comprising of another six halls located to the south and an administration building was completed. In the river valley at the foot of the exhibition center the building was realigned with an open-air theater. The oval theater with approximately 35,000 seats is embedded into a slope and opens up towards the exhibition center, which forms the backdrop for the annual Nanning Folksong Festival.

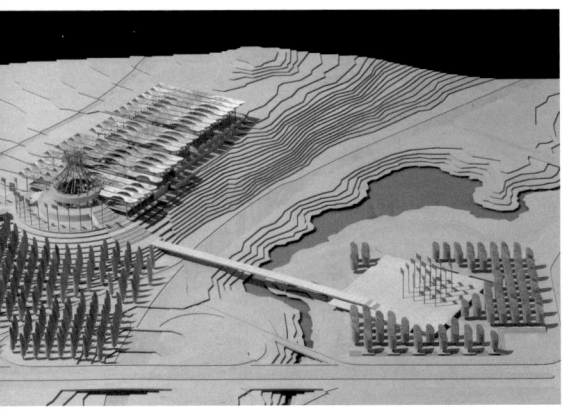

01

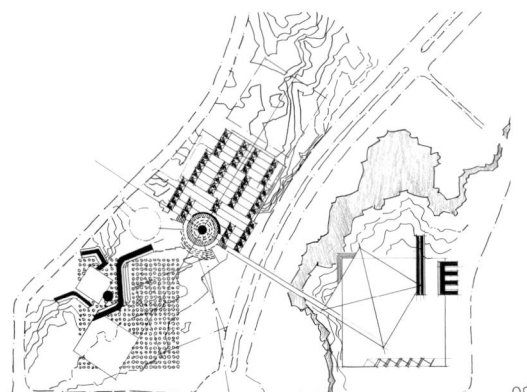

02

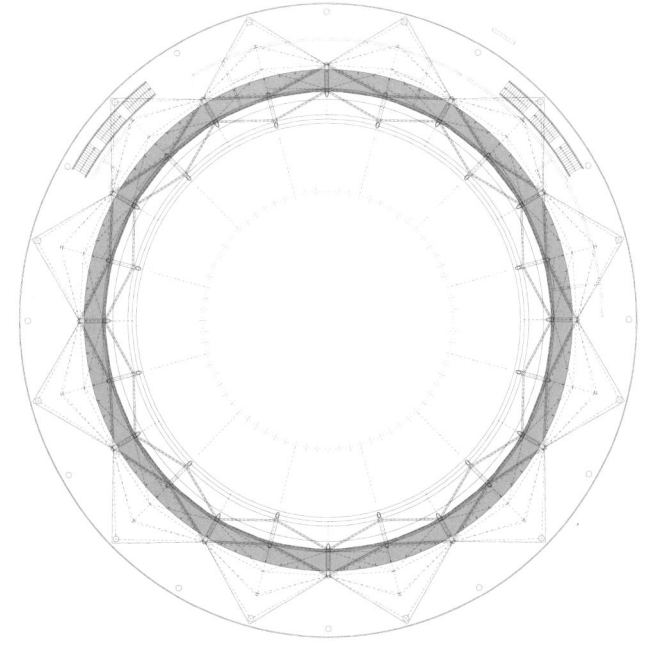

01

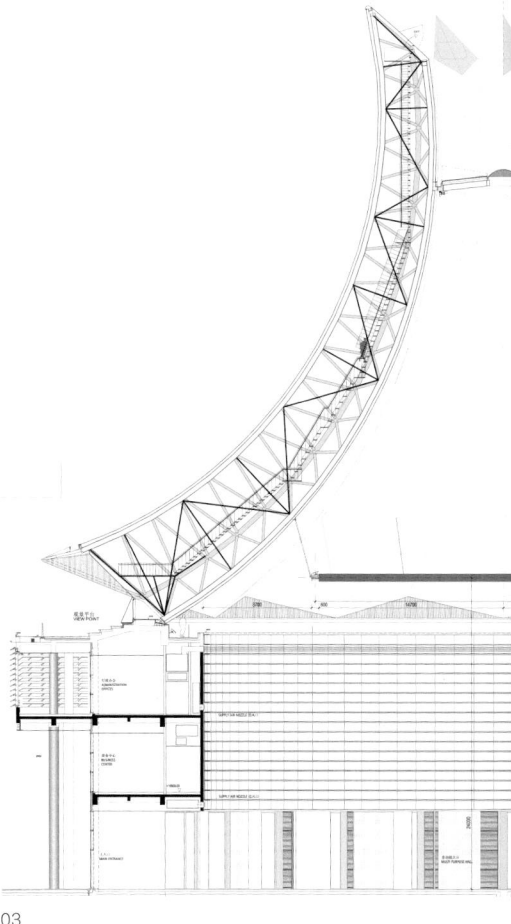

03

02

01 Plan of the roof construction
02 View into the illuminated folded roof construction of the rotunda
03 Detail section of the roof construction

Opposite page
The multifunctional hall forms the head of the exhibition buildings.

Following page
Elevation of the overall complex at night

CONVENTION & EXHIBITION CENTER, SHENZHEN

深圳会展中心

Competition 2001 – 1st prize
Design Volkwin Marg and Nikolaus Goetze
Project managers Marc Ziemons, Thomas Schuster
Design and project team Carsten Plog, Katja Zoschke, Susanne Winter,
Dirk Balser, Sven Greiser, Martin Marschner, Moritz Hoffmann-Becking,
Wei Wu, Martina Klostermann, Iris van Hülst, Flori Wagner, Tina Stahnke,
Marina Hoffmann, Karen Seekamp, Heike Kugele, Otto Dorn, Jeanny Rieger
Light planning Schlotfeld Licht
Chinese partner practice China Northeast Architectural Design
Institute, Shenzhen
Client Shenzhen Convention & Exhibition Center
Gross floor area 256,000 m²
Construction period 2002–2005

01 Longitudinal section
02 View of the main entrance with perron
and fountains

Opposite page
The glass façade seems like a showcase.

Following page
The long horizontal structure forms
a contrast to the predominantly vertical
aesthetic of the numerous high-rise
towers which frame the exhibition center
on both sides.

The building program of the new exhibition center in the young city of Shenzhen
required a considerate synthesis of urban planning, architecture and construction,
thereby achieving an integral structure with an urban density. The total exhibition
area is located on one level with a rectangular plan of approximately 280 m by
540 m. Along the central zone, large A-shaped steel trestle structures are positioned
at intervals of 30 m. These rise to almost 60 m and stem the 360-m-long, 60-m-
wide and 20-m-high congress building to a height of more than 15 m above the
actual hall structure. The A-shaped trestles have a frame-like stiffening and are
interconnected to produce mutual stabilization.

The tube-shaped congress building hovers above the exhibition halls and can be
operated as a separate unit according to the respective demands, with 50 per cent
of its capacity or in combination with the exhibition area. The SZCEC with its length
of more than 540 m is evocative of the famous Crystal Palace of the London World
Exhibition in 1852 and surpasses the large glass hall of the Leipzig Exhibition Center
built in 1996 with double the length.

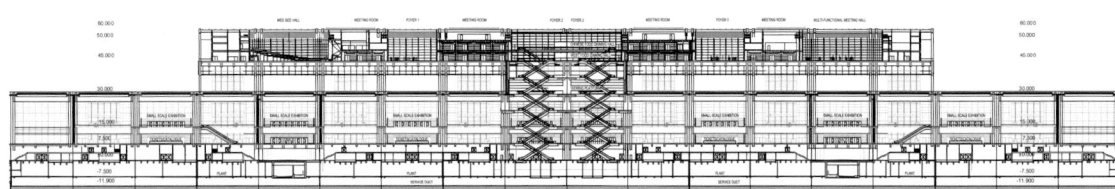

01

02

02

01 Along the hall's central axis, large
A-shaped steel trestle structures
are positioned at 30-m intervals.
They rise to a height of almost 60 m.
02 Interior view of the congress hall
03 Ground floor plan
04 Interior view of the exhibition area

03

04

INTERNATIONAL CONFERENCE AND EXHIBITION CENTER, XI'AN

西安国际会展中心

Competition 2006 – 1st prize
Design Volkwin Marg
Partner Nikolaus Goetze
Project managers Hinrich Müller, Marc Ziemons
Design and project team Christine von der Schulenburg,
Andreas Jantzen, Ben Grope, Tanja Gutena, Carsten Plog, Mei Pan,
Honghao Zhu, Alexandra Kühne, Stephan Berndt, Zhengao Li
Chinese partner practice Architectural Design & Research Inst.
South China University of Technology (SCUT)
Client Xi'an Qujiang Cultural Industry Investment Group
AHB Architectural Design & Engineering Ltd.
Gross floor area 152,000 m²
Construction period 2002–2005

01 The glass front gives the
impression of a showcase.
02 Interior view of one of the
seven new exhibition halls

Opposite page
Exhibition mall

The site for the new Xi'an CEC, which was determined by an existing exhibition hall, is located south of the historical Old City of Xi'an and marks a new area of urban development. Visitors are able to access the seven new exhibition halls, which have the identical measurements of 72 m x 144 m, from the exhibition mall via two entrances. Spacious conference rooms are located in the gallery area which is connected to the ground floor exhibition space by two stairways. The conference rooms also provide a view of the activities in the exhibition space. Through these galleries all the exhibition halls are connected to each other via bridges. On the ground floor the halls are connected additionally to one another via connecting corridors. The barrel-like roof structure of the new exhibition halls is made of steel, giving it impressive light and innovative qualities. The north and south gable façades are glazed, while the long sides are made of a solid concrete skeleton frame construction. The 380-m-long and 42-m-wide exhibition mall is the spine of the exhibition center. Three inner courtyards with outdoor catering invite the visitor to linger and provide the whole exhibition center with a pleasant atmosphere.

01

02

MUSEUM AND ARCHIVE, SHANGHAI-PUDONG

上海浦东文献中心

Competition 2002 – 1st prize
Design Meinhard von Gerkan
Partner Nikolaus Goetze
Project managers Dirk Heller, Karen Schroeder
Design and project team Christoph Berle, Georg Traun, Friedhelm Chlosta, Kai Siebke, Meike Schmidt, Wencke Eissing-Poggenberg, Wei Wu, Holger Wermers, Birgit Föllmer, Hinrich Müller, Udo Meyer, Thomas Eberhardt
Chinese partner practice SIADR, Shanghai Institute of Architectural Design & Research Co., Ltd.
Client City of Shanghai, New District Pudong
Gross floor area 41,000 m²
Construction period 2003–2006

The museum documents and archives the history and development of the new district Pudong. Modern, multifunctional and open exhibition spaces are developed to inform the public with a permanent exhibition and special exhibitions about selected topics of the city's history. Three elements form the building complex: the square-shaped main building, a much broader 4-m-high base with surrounding stairs which accommodates the archives and an administration tract. Two parallel façade-layers form the façade of the upper closed part of the main building. The outer layer consists of glass and the inner one of room-high closed wall panels. These elements can be rotated along their longitudinal axis and can be opened or closed according to the requirements of the exhibition concept so that views from the inside to the outside and vice versa are generated.

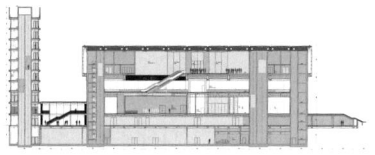

01

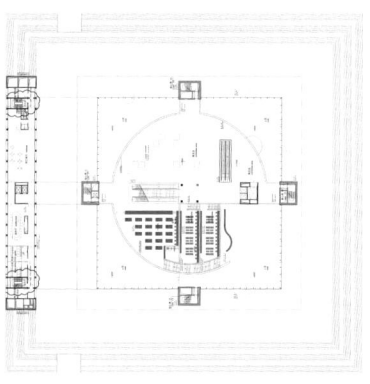

02

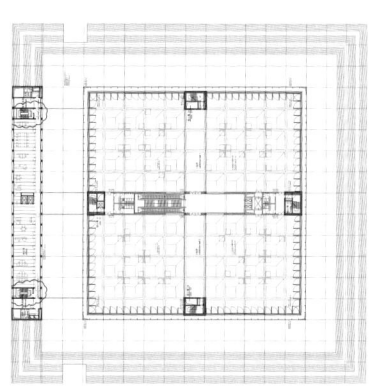

03

04

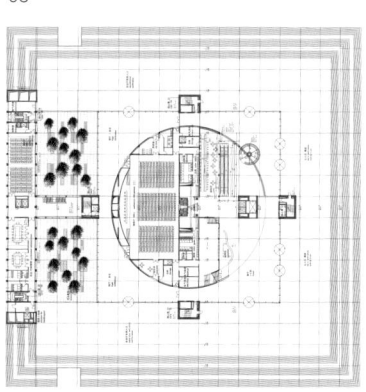

05

01 Section
02 Basement
03 First floor
04 First story
05 Second story

Opposite page
The plasticity of the disk-molded façade in contrast to the horizontal orientation

Following page
The load-bearing construction is recognizable behind the glass front.

01

02

03

04

ZHONGGUANCUN CHRISTIAN CHURCH, HAIDIAN DISTRICT, BEIJING

北京海淀区中关村基督教堂

Competition 2004 – 1st prize
Design Meinhard von Gerkan
Partner Stephan Schütz
Design and project team Stephan Rewolle, Xia Lin, Helga Reimund,
Gero Heimann, Katrin Kanus, Ralf Sieber, Gregor Hoheisel
Chinese partner practice Sunlight
Client China Zhongguancun Culture Development Co., Ltd.
Gross floor area 4,000 m²
Construction period 2005–2007

This design for the largest Christian church in China is characterized by
a Chinese type of "triple p", meaning public-private partnership with
commercial spaces on the ground floor, and by its striking façade rod
system. With its free curved shape the building forms a solitaire in the
open space between the Zhongguancun Cultural Tower and the "city of
books". The shape of the church body made it possible to keep open
the sightline to the south media façade of the Cultural Tower and to
create equally dynamic open spaces through to the surrounding
buildings. The symbol of the cross, identifying the building as a
Christian church, develops from the façade rod system. Through a
large portal-type door worshippers mount a stairway to enter the main
church hall on the first upper floor. Here they turn east towards the
altar. With its alternation of openings and massive wall sections, the
façade rod system creates a special lighting atmosphere matching
the ecclesiastical function of the space.

01 The Christian Church
beside the Cultural Tower
02 Section
03 Northeast elevation

Opposite page
The envelope of the
church is characterized
by a vertical concrete
rod system.

01

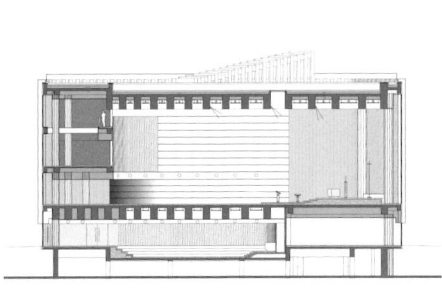

02

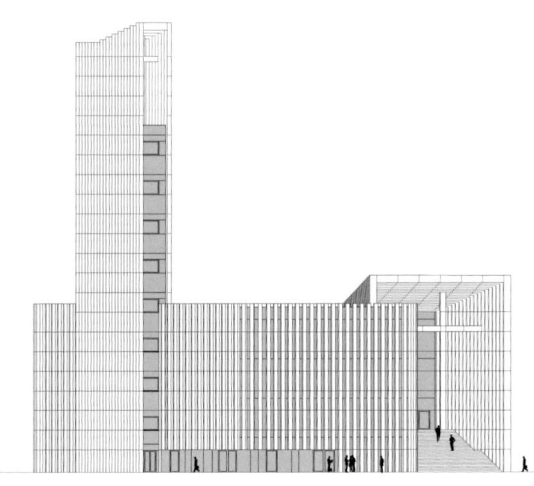

03

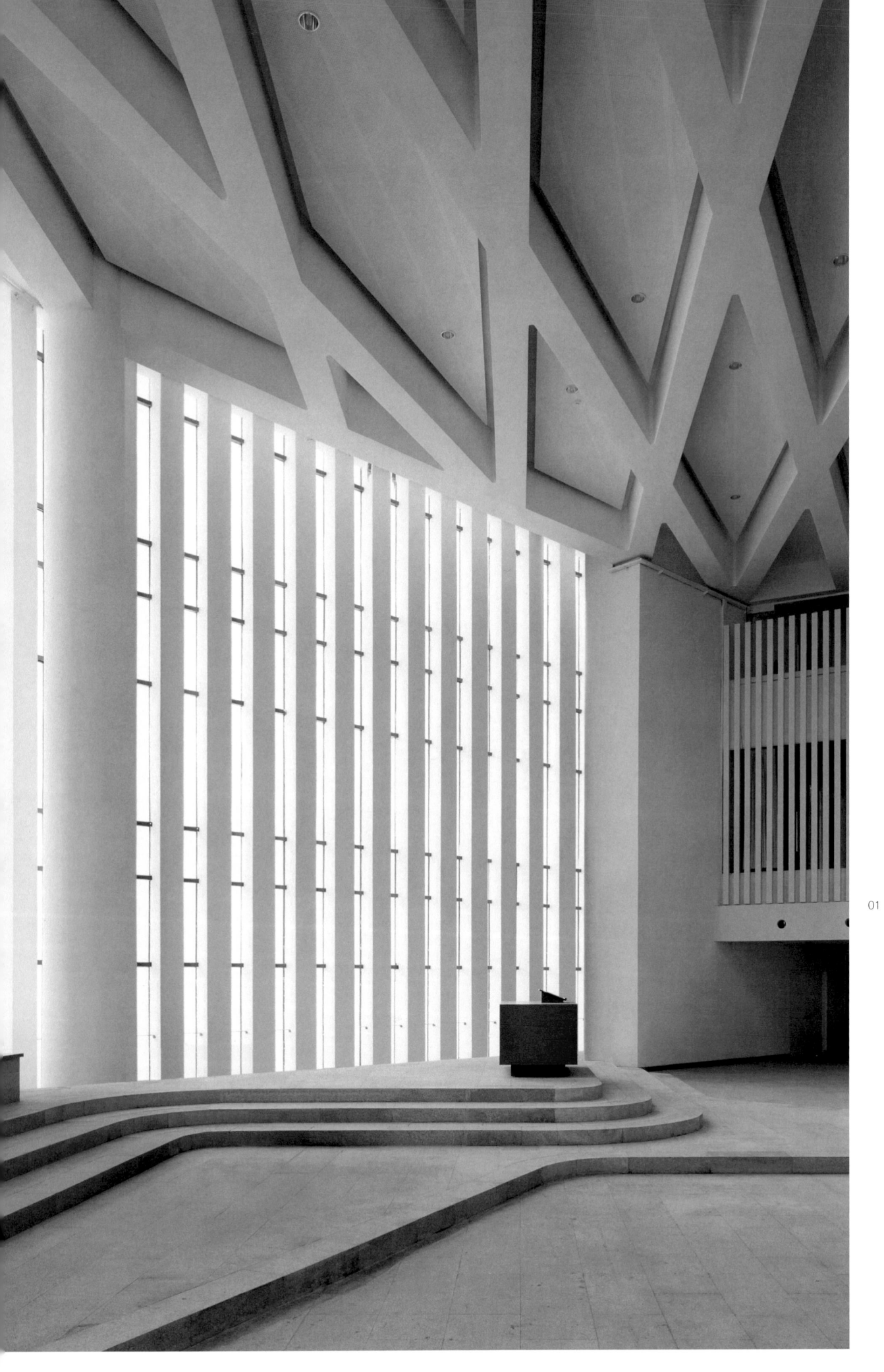

02

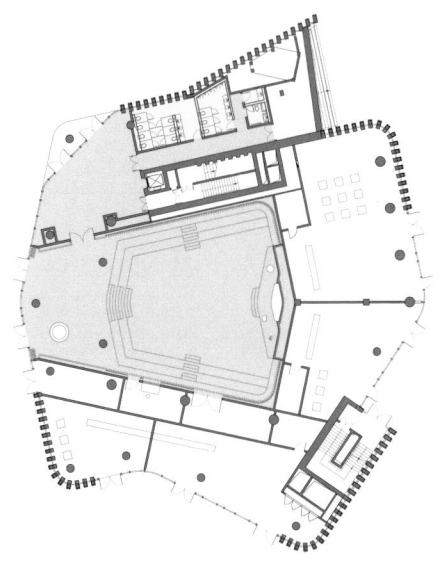

03

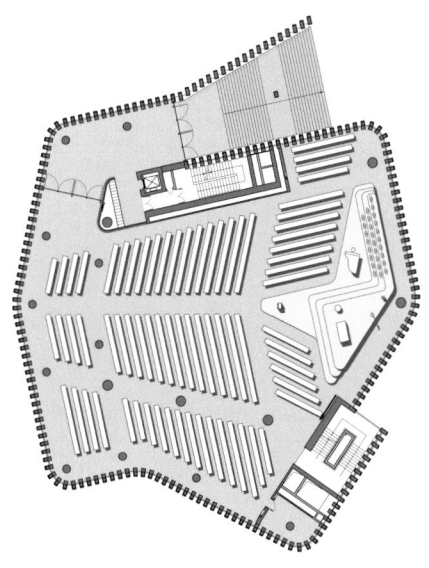

04

01 Interior view detail with pulpit
02 View into the nave
03 Plan level 0
04 Plan level 4

Following page
The open roof girder
construction produces an
organic ceiling painting.

ZHONGGUANCUN CULTURAL CENTER, BEIJING

北京中关村文化商厦

Competition 2002 – 1st prize
Design Meinhard von Gerkan
Partner Stephan Schütz
Project manager Nicolas Pomränke
Design and project team Doris Schäffler, Gero Heimann, Xia Lin, Giuseppina Orto, Jan Pavuk, Margret Böthig
Structural engineers Schlaich, Bergermann and Partners
Chinese partner practice Sunlight Architects & Engineers Co., Ltd.
Client China Zhongguancun Culture Development Co., Ltd.
Gross floor area 85,000 m²
Height 80 m
Floors 17
Construction period 2003–2006

Surrounding glass strips enclose the building in a seemingly flowing movement. In response to the inner courtyards the façade possesses curvilinear setbacks which follow the trapezoidal plan and present great plasticity. At the same time the deliberate modelling of the glass strips characterizes the entrances. Sharp-edged cornice profiles generate a vertical structure on the glass façade. Images can be projected onto the façades with the support of mirrors, making the building appear at night a symbol of modern media technology.
The large public areas of the cultural center are accessed via a mall in north-south direction which offers a generous gallery space on the first six floors. The hall of the internal building part opens to the eastern road. This V-shaped space evokes a unique atmosphere which is further increased by light and sound installations. The roof level is designed as a business center with restaurants, bars, discotheques and terraces. At a height of 80 m visitors enjoy the panoramic view over Beijing.

01 Site plan

Opposite page
Detail of the "screen"-façade

01

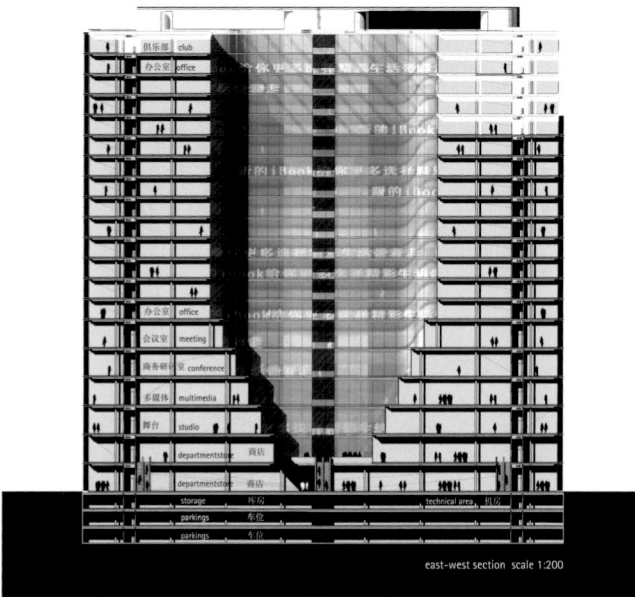

east-west section scale 1:200

01

01 Section
02 Section through the lamella
structure used as projection plan
03 Projection onto the façades with
the support of mirrors

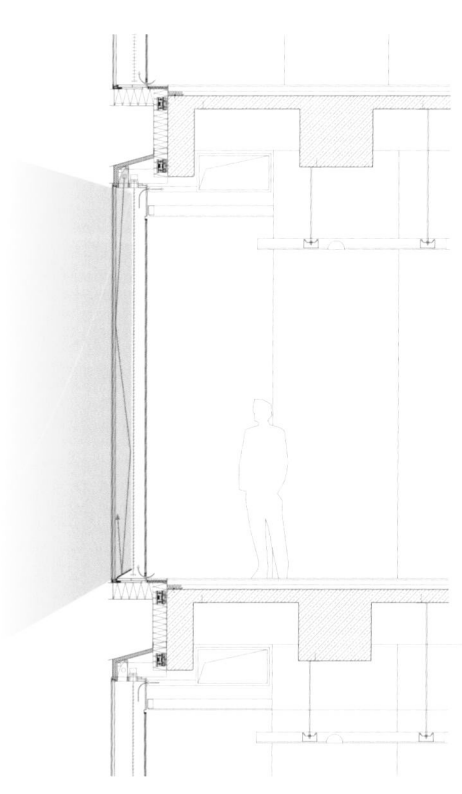

02

01

01 View of the round staircase
   well with the elevators
02 Daylight illuminates the corridors.

DEVELOPMENT CENTRAL BUILDING, GUANGZHOU

广州发展中心大厦

Competition 2001 – 1st prize
Design Meinhard von Gerkan and Nikolaus Goetze
with Volkmar Sievers
Design and project team Simone Nentwig, Huan Zhu,
Jörn Bohlmann, Robert Wildegger, Tilo Günther, Lars Neininger,
Andrea Moritz, Tobias Plinke, Heike Kugele, Nils Dethlefs, Knut Maass
Structural engineers Ove Arup & Partners
Chinese partner practice GZDI, Guangzhou Design Institute
Client Guangzhou Developing New City Investment Co., Ltd.
Gross floor area 78,600 m²
Height 150 m
Floors 37
Construction period 2002–2005

01 Ground floor plan

Opposite page
The illuminated exterior
sun-screening metal
lamellas give a bizarre
look to the building.

The predominant position of this building on the Pearl River underlines
its importance amongst the whole variety of tower buildings. All office
units are optimally lit due to the narrow building depth. This is achieved
by dividing the building into three sections – a glassed midsection with
a central area of access and two flanking slightly narrower side
sections where the offices are located. The side section façades are
structured with a grid pattern made up of supports with natural stone
facing, and cross beams, integrating two stories.
Vertical sun-screening metal lamellas which are electrically controlled
move according to the position of the sun. They provide for glare-free
light and a pleasant temperature in the offices. The interior of the building is characterized by a small number of high-quality materials. In
addition to natural stone, glass and wood, it is above all characterized
by the facing on the central core of the building, which is made of jade
green textured glass.

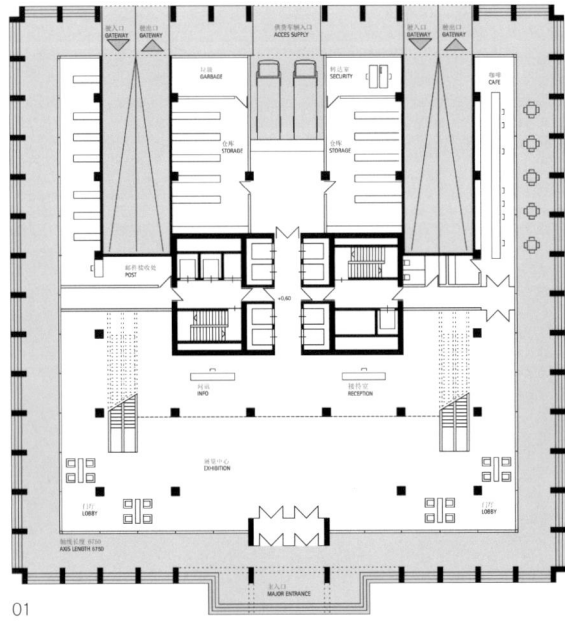

01

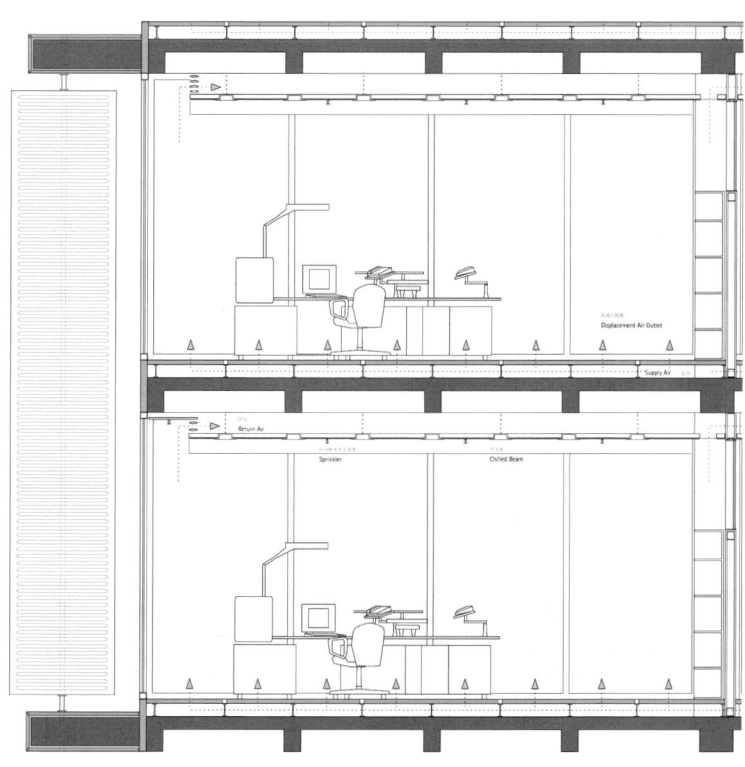

01

01 View of the lobby
02 Façade section

Opposite page
Detail of the exterior vertical
sun-screening lamellas

Displacement Air Outlet

Supply Air

Return Air

Sprinkler   Chilled Beam

GONG YUAN BUILDING, HANGZHOU

杭州公元大厦

Design Meinhard von Gerkan, 2003
Partner Nikolaus Goetze
Project manager Volkmar Sievers
Design and project team Simone Nentwig, Huan Zhu, Andrea Moritz, Knut Maass, Rouven Oberdiek, Tobias Plinke, Nicole Loeffler, Wiebke Dorn, Nils Dethlefs, Kerstin Steinfatt, Jörn Bohlmann
Chinese partner practice ZADRI
Client Hangzhou Nice Source United Real Estate Co., Ltd.
Gross floor area 123,000 m²
Construction period 2003–2006

The Gong Yuan office building is located in the immediate vicinity of the Huanglong Stadium in Hangzhou. It functions as a representative entrance to the sports center on the opposite side of the street and is simultaneously a cornerstone in the prospering district of the city. Two groups of high-rise buildings, each with a striking tripartite division, occupy the north and south ends of the property. An enclosed green courtyard bordered on the east and west sides by colonnades stretches between the two towers. A four-level press center in the form of a glass rotunda pierces the northern end of the western colonnade.

01 Site plan
02 View over the building complex with its green courtyard bordered by colonnades and the press center

Opposite page
Symbiosis between the severe vertical façade and the landscape gardening

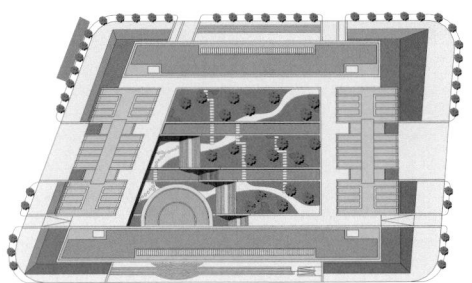

01

02

01 Enclosed green courtyard
  with water basins and
  colonnades
02 Colonnades at night

02

01

02

03

DIXINGJU OFFICE BUILDING, BEIJING

北京地兴居写字楼

Consultancy 2003
Design Meinhard von Gerkan with Doris Schäffler and Stephan Schütz
Design and project team David Schenke, Chunsong Dong
Chinese partner practice CABR, Building Design Institute – China
Academy of Building Research
Client Beijing Shoulu-Huayuan Property Co., Ltd.
Gross floor area 33,000 m²
Construction period 2004–2006

Despite the comparatively low height that was required by the local
authorities the building creates an impressive silhouette to the 2nd
Ring Road via a glass hall as the center of the ensemble consisting of
a singular office building to the west and four office volumes in a
windmill-like structure to the east. On three sides of the site horizontal
louvers surround the complex providing ideal sun protection and
furthermore individual courtyards.

01 View to the courtyard
02 Site plan

Opposite page
The façade is characterized
by horizontal lamellas with
rounded corners.

Following page
Colonnades in harmony with
light and water

01

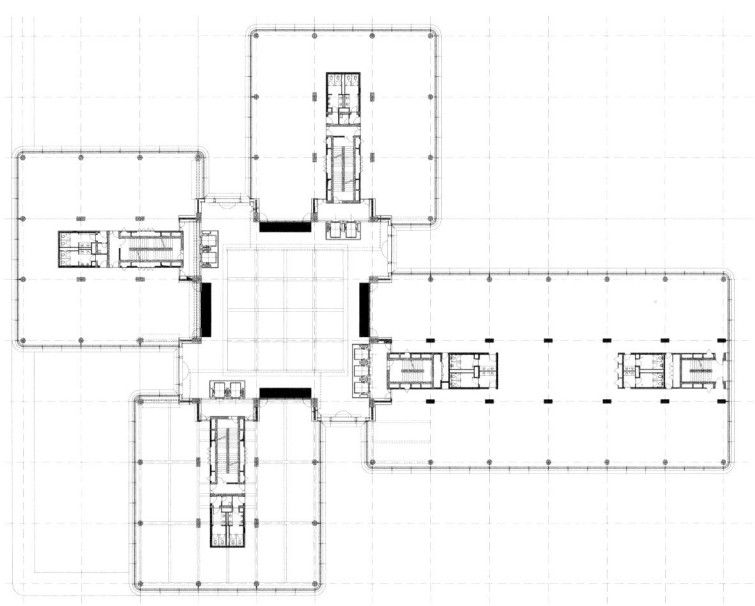

02

北京文华艺术中心

Competition 2003
Design Meinhard von Gerkan and Stephan Schütz
Project management David Schenke, Lin Lin Jiang
Design and project team Ralf Sieber, Na Zhang, Ran Li,
Daniela Franz
Chinese partner practice Jianghe Group
Client Beijing Oriental Continent Real Estate Development and
Management Co., Ltd.
Gross floor area 140,000 m^2
Construction period 2006–2008

The Orient Wenhua Art Center is situated on Beijing's eastern-lying
second ring road at the intersection between the city's historical
quarter and the new business and office district of modern Beijing.
The complex, which is accessed via a podium level, is made up of a
5-star hotel with 520 rooms, a cultural center and an office building.
By means of an expansive set of stairs, the podium connects the two
neighborhoods with one other, as well as providing the spatial situation
to accommodate the hotel's and office building's entrance halls.
The culture hall – a small but important structure – is framed by the
other volumes and is situated in the middle of the complex, helping to
stress its significance. The hall's façade is made of several layers of
gold-colored rods which by means of varied reflections of light coming
from different angles create a structured yet transparent golden
casing. The façades of the hotel and office building are built of glass
and aluminum panel elements which can be quickly mounted on the
building site thanks to their high level of prefabrication.

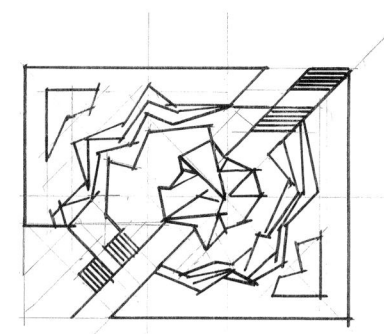

01

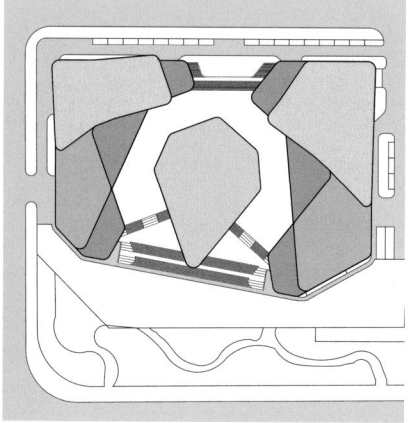

02

01 Concept sketch
02 Site plan of the modified
design planning
03 The "golden" exhibition hall
is situated in the middle of
the complex.

Opposite page
View into the glazed lobby

03

BEIJING CHÂTEAU, BEIJING

北京公馆

Design Meinhard von Gerkan with Magdalene Weiß, 2002
Partner Nikolaus Goetze
Design and project team Michèle Watenphul, Kai Ladebeck,
Holger Schmücker, Xia Lin, Gregor Hoheisel, Stephanie Heß,
Iris van Hülst, Sigrid Müller, Jörn Ortmann, Marcus Tanzen,
Hito Ueda, Holger Wermers
Chinese partner practice Central Research Institute of
Building and Construction Design of M.M.I
Client Beijing Shoulu-Huayuan Property Co., Ltd.
Gross floor area 69,000 m^2
Construction period 2003–2008

01 Ground floor plan with lobby,
swimming pool, beauty salon,
bar and restaurant
02 One of Beijing's first double
façades on a residential building

Opposite page
Vertical layers and constructed
bands give scale and dimension
to the building.

Beijing, once at the heart of the Chinese empire, is now a political,
economic and cultural center and the focus of the world's attention. As
the first private luxury apartment building, the elegant Beijing Château
rises clearly above its metropolitan surroundings in the middle of this
multicultural cosmopolitan city. It epitomizes the realization of the
unusual and demanding task to develop a unique high-end residential
building composed of stacked "villas".

The building with its rounded, glassy, gleaming metallic double façade
appears like a structural sculpture at the heart of this administrative
and embassy district. The outward appearance follows on the inside in
elegant two-storied apartments that offer a maximum of quality and
lifestyle including a panoramic view from each. At the same time
integrated wooden sunscreens allow individually controlled spatial
closure. The shape of the building produces 80 diverse, extremely
individual apartment types, all with terraces and large outside spaces.
1000 m^2 luxury apartments in the top floors supply flexibly divisible
living areas with swimming pools.

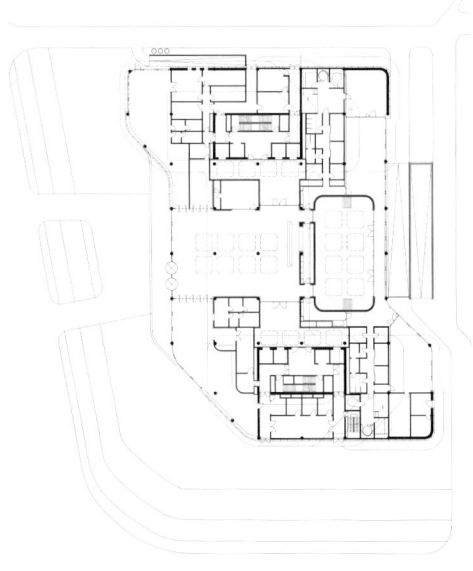

01

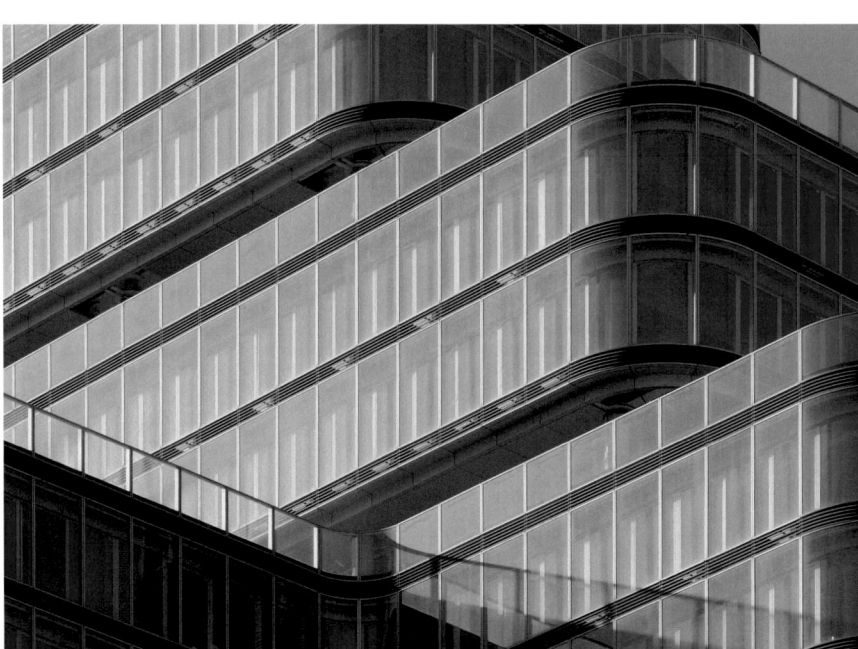

02

CYTS TOWER, BEIJING

北京中青旅大厦

Design Meinhard von Gerkan with Stephan Schütz
and Doris Schäffler, 2003
Design and project team Nicolas Pomränke, Giuseppina Orto,
Chen Lan, Anette Löber, Ralf Sieber
Structural engineers Schlaich, Bergermann and Partners
Chinese partner practice CABR
Client China CYTS Tours Holding Co., Ltd.
Gross floor area 65,000 m²
Construction period 2004–2006

The clear structural order of the office building of "China Youth Travel Service" is
directly related to the philosophy of one of the biggest travel companies in China:
clear and transparent yet innovative and efficient at the same time. Bridges and
observer elevators are placed within the two 75-m-high atriums so that the space
and the view of the city landscape can be physically experienced by both visitors and
employees. The center part of the building is determined by four-story-high halls.
These spaces serve as communication zones for all the people working in this
CYTS building and also grant a view of the city. With lush greenery these zones
provide a pleasant atmosphere. The building's façade consists of a dark aluminium
structure, giving the building a strong proportion. In Summer 2007 gmp opened their
Beijing office in this building.

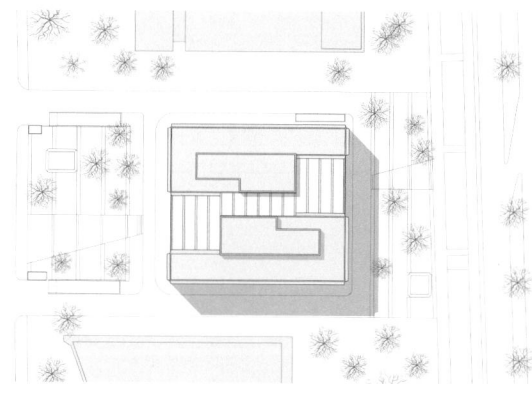

02

01 Main entrance –
The gmp branch-office is
located on the 11th story
02 Site plan

Opposite page
The plasticity of the façade
is intensified by the depth.

01

01

01 View through the cable-glass
façade to Chinese buildings with
"cocktail cherries" on the top
02 The natural stone façade provides
for a warm atmosphere in the
interior.

Following page
Interpenetration of light and shade

WANDA PLAZA, HOTEL AND OFFICE COMPLEX, BEIJING
北京万达广场

Competition 2002 – 1st prize
Design Volkwin Marg and Hubert Nienhoff
Project managers Alexander Buchhofer, Silvia Schneider
Design team Christian Dorndorf, Martin Duplantier, Xia Lin,
Nicolas Pomränke
Project team (Façade design) Veit Lieneweg, Stefan Rewolle,
Du Peng, Chunsong Dong
Chinese partner practice Jianghe Group
Client Wanda Plaza Property Co., Ltd.
Gross floor area 130,000 m²
Construction period 2005–2007

The two structures are to be understood as abstract stone sculptures from which
vertical towers (hotel and office use) are developed out of a horizontal base (commercial use). The two buildings create a striking entity within the heterogeneous
urban fabric by means of the towers' distinctive projection into the urban area around
Jianguo Road. Setback floors as well as large-scale recesses at the entrances to the
towers act to organize the building. Shaded colonnades form the structure's base
zone. The façade's natural materials – granulated granite of a light, warm color – reflect the sunlight and draw attention to the building ensemble. The deep reveals and
the sculptural effect of the architectural bodies thereby allow a staged image of light
and shade to emerge that emphasizes the overall form's effect in the
urban environment.

01

02

01 Façade elevation with
cantilevered head construction
02 Site plan

Opposite page
2–3 stories are situated behind
each horizontal façade zoning.

Following page
The symmetry and severity of
the façade structure create
a distinctive projection into the
urban area around Jianguo
Road.

CENTURY LOTUS SPORTS PARK WITH STADIUM AND SWIMMING HALL, FOSHAN

佛山世纪莲体育中心〔体育场和游泳馆〕

Competition 2003 – 2nd prize
Design Volkwin Marg with Christian Hoffmann
Partner Nikolaus Goetze
Project manager Christian Hoffmann
Design team Marek Nowak, Christoph Helbich, Mario Rojas Toledo, Michael König, Sven Greiser, Sebastian Hilke, Mark Jackschat
Project team Michael Haase, Stephan Menke, Franz Lensing, Björn Füchtenkord, Sven Greiser, Silke Flaßnöcker, Ebi Tang, Jennifer Kielas
Structural engineers Schlaich, Bergermann and Partners
Client Foshan Sports Site Construction Center for the 12th Provincial Sports Event
Chinese partner practice South China University, Architectural Design and Research Institute
Seats stadium: 36,000; swimming hall: 2,800
Construction period 2004–2006

The stadium is situated in the park like a flourishing water rose in a lake. Being situated on a hill it forms the new landmark of the park on the river and adds an imposing and monumental shape to the southern cityscape of the new Foshan. The stadium roof unfolds itself with its white membrane like a radiant bloom. With 120 x 180 m being the biggest retractable roof in the world it turns the stadium into one of the biggest fully-covered arenas in the world within twelve minutes. When the stadium is uncovered, the whole inner roof disappears in a big video-cube that is floating above the center of the sports field. The roof of the swimming hall is as well covered by a lightweight and translucent membrane roof. Embedded in the landscape it takes up the architectural design idea, creating the strong impression of the two buildings as an architectural ensemble.

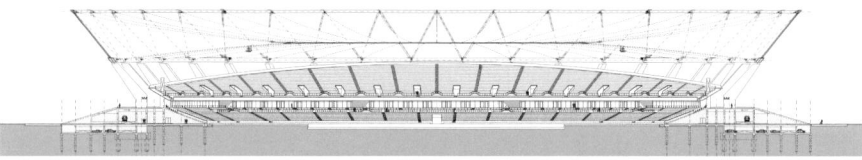

01

01 Longitudinal section of the access gallery between the upper and lower levels
02 Interior view of the stadium

Opposite page
Master plan – Track and field stadium with football field and swimming pool

Following page
The stadium stands out as a landmark with its white mobile roof.

02

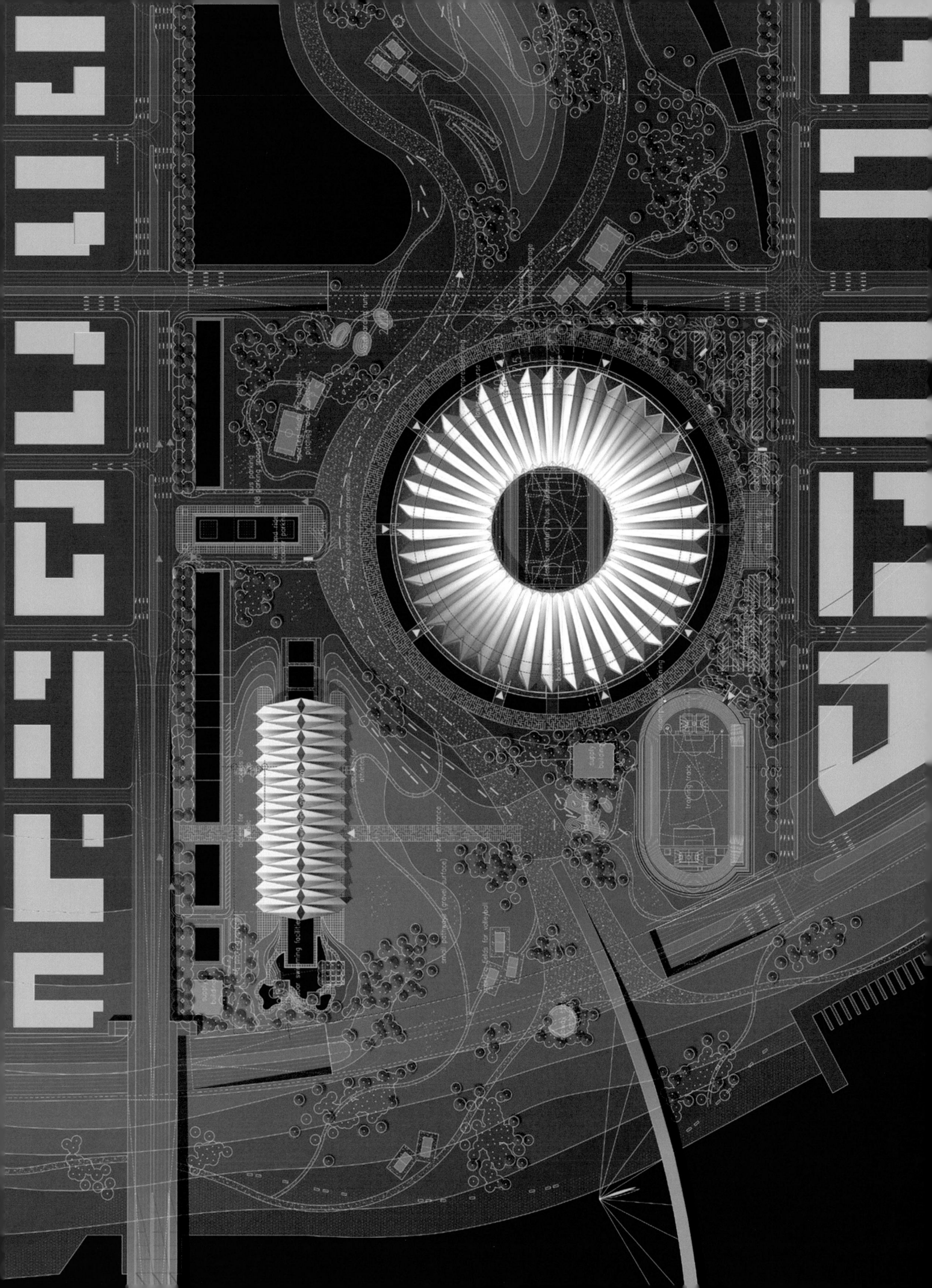

01

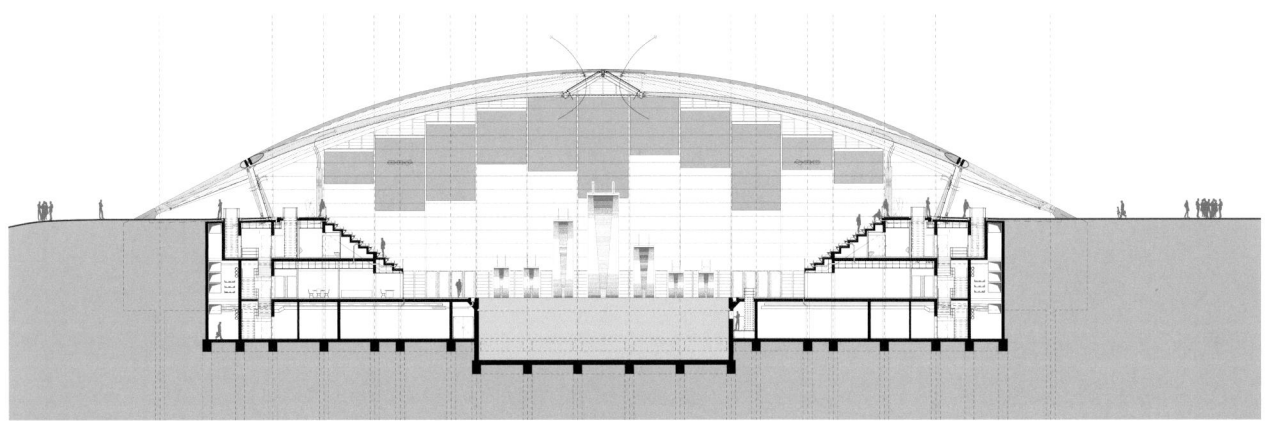

02

01 The translucent membrane roof appears
   to hover unsupported above the water.
02 Section of the swimming hall
03 Supporting structure
04 The stands and pools are embedded
   into the plateau of dike topography.

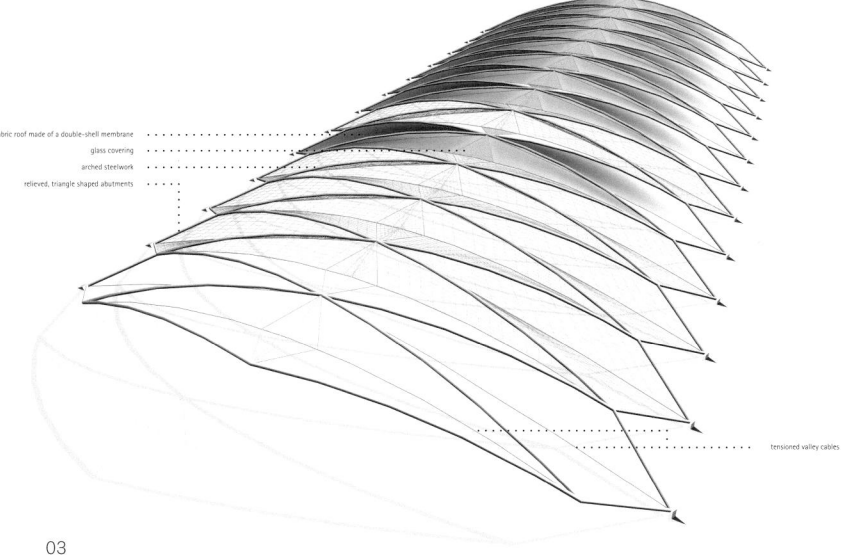

fabric roof made of a double-shell membrane
glass covering
arched steelwork
relieved, triangle shaped abutments

tensioned valley cables

03

04

01

BASKETBALL CENTER, DONGGUAN

东莞篮球中心

Competition 2006 – 1st prize
Design Meinhard von Gerkan and Stephan Schütz
Project management Stephan Rewolle
Design team Katina Roloff, Patrick Pfleiderer, Matthias Wiegelmann, Chunsong Dong, Bin Zhou, Yan Liu, Yue Wang, Jun Li, Lu Han, Ping Cao, Linda Stannieder, Li Yang, Chaojie Yin
Structural engineers Schlaich, Bergermann and Partners
Chinese partner practice CABR
Client Dongguan Civil Construction Administration Office
Gross floor area 60,600 m²
Seats 14,730
Construction period 2006–2009

01 Ground floor plan
02 Interior view of the foyer

Opposite page
Bird's eye view and sketch (bottom)

Due to its location in the southwest of Liaobu Town the Dongguan Basketball Center occupies a highly prominent position in the city context. The overall goal of the design is to define the sports center as a landmark. Therefore the gymnasium is perceived as the epicenter of the entire basketball city. The structural order of the project is clear and simple in order to set a reasonable framework for the different development steps. The plaza is determined by two high-rise buildings containing a hotel and an office tower. The gymnasium's roof consists of a cable structure which allows the use of a minimum of steel. The roof is clad with a textile PFTE material, so that daylight is provided to the space without any glare. Due to the daylight the gymnasium can be operated economically as the illumination is exclusively necessary at nighttime. In order to provide a sufficient insulation the underside of the roof construction is clad with PFTE as well so that a big cavity is produced which can be illuminated at nighttime.

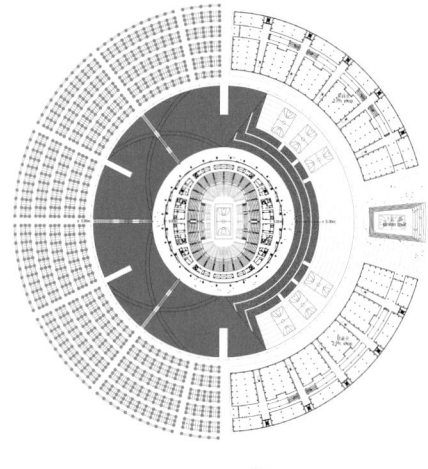

01

02

BAO'AN STADIUM, SHENZHEN

深圳宝安体育场

Competition 2007, 1st prize
Design Meinhard von Gerkan and Stephan Schütz
Design team David Schenke, Jennifer Heckenlaible, Daniela Franz,
Ran Li, Xi Zhang, Bin Zhou, Chao Jie Yin, Anna Bulanda-Jansen,
Zhan Yu
Client The Sports Bureau of Bao'an District, Shenzhen
Gross floor area 88,500 m²
At planning stage

In 2011 Shenzhen will host the second-largest sporting event world-wide – the Universiade Games. Within the context of this venue, the newly built Bao'an Stadium will serve as the location for football competitions. In order to create a landmark building it is the overall target of the architectural design of the Bao'an Stadium project to combine the cheerful spirit of these games with local features of Shenzhen and the south of China. Therefore a "bamboo forest" – the plant which symbolizes the south of China – is chosen as a picture for the design and is being transformed into architecture. In the design of the stadium green-colored columns all around the concourse create an irregular pattern of light and shadow while carrying the load of the roof as well as the load of the stands at the same time. The spectators move through these columns and arrive at the top of the lower stands where a breathtaking view of the inside of the stadium is provided.

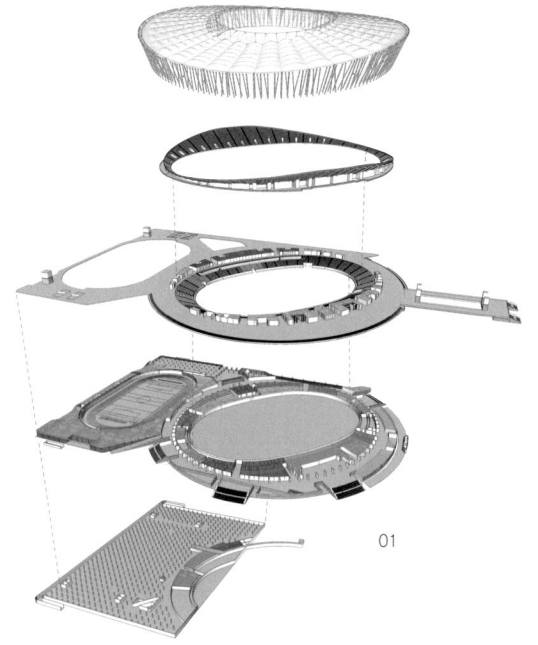

01

01 Functional schematic
02 + Opposite page
  A distinctive feature are the
  bamboo-like columns.

02

NATIONAL MUSEUM OF CHINA, BEIJING

北京国家博物馆

Competition 2004 – 1st prize
Design Meinhard von Gerkan with Stephan Schütz,
Stephan Rewolle and Doris Schäffler
Design team Gregor Hoheisel, Katrin Kanus, Ralf Sieber,
Du Peng, Chunsong Dong
Project team Matthias Wiegelmann, Patrick Pfleiderer,
Helga Reimund, Tobias Keyl, Anna Bulanda, Christian Dorndorf,
Ulli Bachmann, Ajda Guelbahar, Johanna Enzinger,
Verena Fischbach, Wei Bao, Yang Liu, Lin Xia
Chinese partner practice CABR
Client National Museum of China
Gross floor area 170,000 m²
Construction period 2007–2010

The National Museum of China is the union of the former "Chinese History Museum" and the "Chinese Revolutionary Museum" and thus the showcase of the history and culture of one of the oldest cultures of mankind. The new building is sited at the cultural and political center of China, the "Square of Heavenly Peace", opposite the "Forbidden City" and the "Great Hall of the People". The focal point of the design is the sensitive integration of the 170,000-m²-large new building in this world famous square ensemble using several parts of the existing museum. The current building offers generosity and dignity via the building-high colonnades, but at the same time it lacks openness and transparency inside because it is blocked by the central entrance building. The comprehensive museum is symbolized by a roof volume which covers the public space and provides weather protection for the people occupying the space. The eave of the roof is located at a height of 34.50 m so that the "Great Hall of People" and the National Museum of China are balanced in height and proportion.

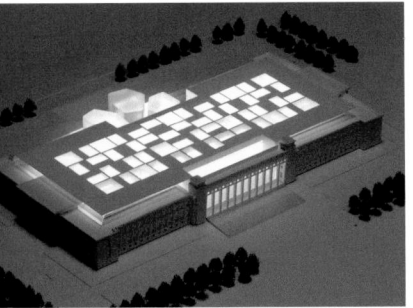

01

01 Model
02 "Square of Heavenly Peace" with view onto the "Forbidden City", the "Great Hall of the People" (on the left), the "Mao Mausoleum" at the center and the National Museum of China (on the right)

Opposite page
Detail elevation of the interior

02

CHINA SCIENCE & TECHNOLOGY MUSEUM, BEIJING

中国科技博物馆

Competition 2005 – 1st prize (without commissioning)
Design Meinhard von Gerkan with Stephan Schütz and Stephan Rewolle
Design team Katrin Kanus, Ralf Sieber, Bin Zhou, Peng Du, David Schenke, Chun Song Dong, Na Zhang, Liu Leyi, Liu Zhihui, Iris Belle, Beidi Meng
Client Chinese Science Technology Institute
Gross floor area 105,000 m²

Situated at the parameter of the Olympic Park the volume of the new China Science and Technology Museum appears like a big-sized stone which is fully integrated in the broad landscape of the park. Stones can be regarded as the most impressive symbols for science and technology since they were the first tools used by human beings. The central space of the building is an airy hall which surrounds the dome-like cinema. This central hall extends from the basement to the top floor so that natural light is provided to the public areas on the level at −8.00 m. The above ground functions are located around five triangular cores. The triangular form of these cores reflect the expressive appearance of the building skin which is produced by triangular surfaces in order to produce a clearly recognizable metaphor of the stone. The triangular surfaces of the façade are subdivided into smaller units and carry a prismatic façade system. The building skin is a modular and prefabricated system which could be flexibly equipped with glass surfaces in those parts of the building where daylight is needed. Due to the orientation of the glass planes direct daylight and sun radiation is avoided which at the same time avoids overheating in summertime. The highly insulated metal panels of the building skin produce a low energy building which can be seen as a pilot project in China.

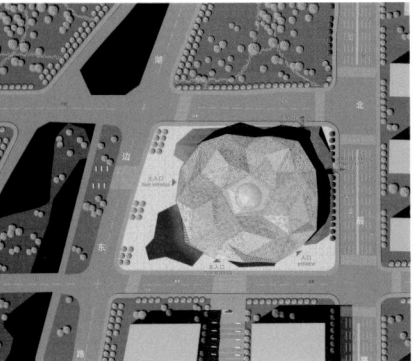

01

01 Site plan / Master plan
02 Function scheme
03 Each core is regularly surrounded by pine triangular ceiling slabs.

Opposite page
The structure of the building is determined by the metaphor of the stone, a crystalline order of minerals.

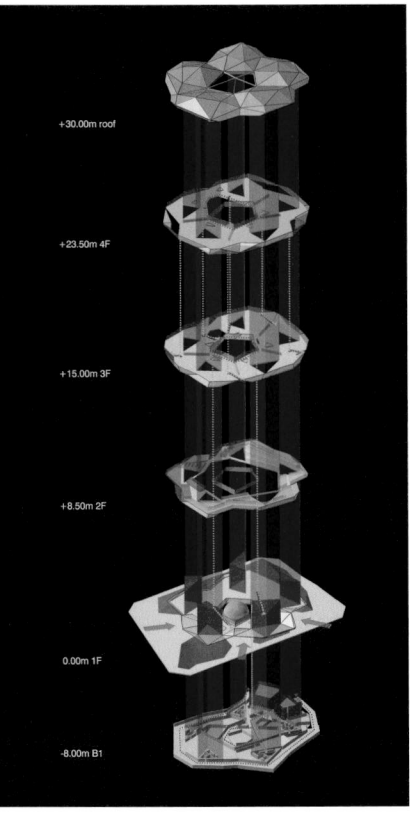

+30.00m roof
+23.50m 4F
+15.00m 3F
+8.50m 2F
0.00m 1F
-8.00m B1

02

03

MUSEUM FOR CULTURE, FINE ARTS AND SCIENCE, CHANGCHUN

长春科技文化综合中心博物馆、美术馆、科技馆综合体

Competition 2006 – 1st prize
Design Meinhard von Gerkan
Partner Nikolaus Goetze
Project management Hinrich Müller, Marc Ziemons
Design and project team Christine von der Schulenburg, Andreas Jantzen, Katrin Loeser, Sven Grotheer, Katja Siebke, Kristina Milani, Tanja Gutena, Heiko Thiess, Dirk Seyffert, Pan Mei, Anna Rzymelka, Ben Grope, Markus Carlsen
Chinese partner practice JPADI, Jilin Provincial Architecture Design Institute Co., Ltd.
Client Changchun Science and Culture Center Project Leading Team
Gross floor area 107,500 m²
Construction period 2007–2009

The three stone cubes housing the three museums are positioned around a common foyer in the shape of a windmill. The structure is symbolic for the integration of the three different museums into one museum complex. The design of each cube has a shape of broken soil in a deep canyon. This symbolizes the history and culture of Jilin Province. The plan of the Fine Arts Museum is designed like a modern painting: clear lines cut the different surfaces. The projection into the third dimension creates the sculptural cube. The plan of the Science Museum contains different sized squares: a rational and geometric form which symbolizes technique and science. The three museums have the same site development idea: sunscreened exhibition spaces arranged along the visitors' tour. The rooms are linked by open bridges which ease the comfort orientation within the buildings and offer a wide view over the museum's park.

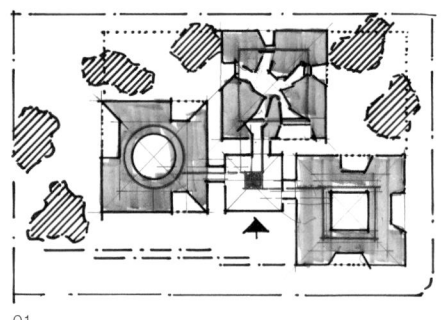

01

01 Sketch by Meinhard von Gerkan
02 Elevation and ground floor plan

Opposite page
Perron to the forecourt of the museum

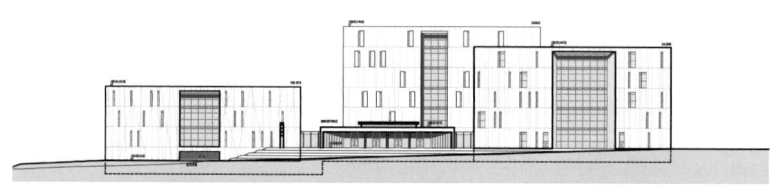

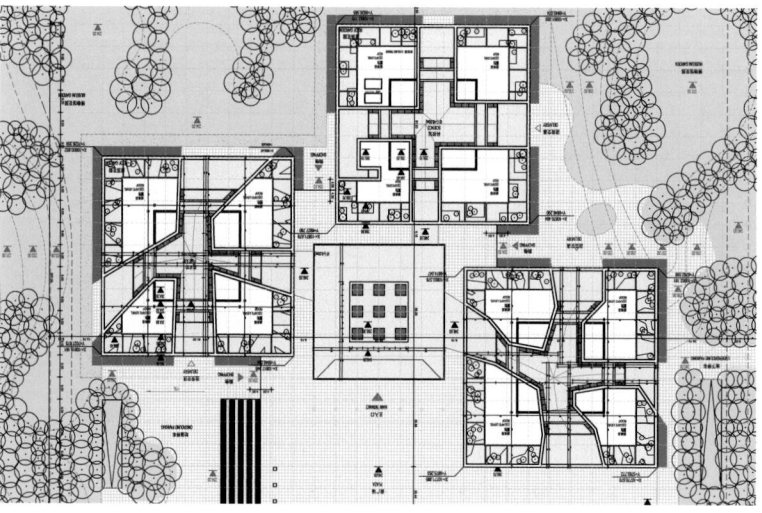

02

WEST RAILWAY STATION, TIANJIN

天津西站

Competition 2004 – 1st prize
Design Meinhard von Gerkan and Stephan Schütz with Nicolas Pomränke
Design team Ralf Sieber, Xu Ji, Jochen Sültrup, Christian Dorndorf, Bernd Gotthardt, Sabine Stage, Cai Wei
Client TSDI Tianjin Ministry of Railway
Gross floor area 52,386 m² (aboveground)

The site of the new Tianjin West Railway Station is located close to the former station whose terminal building belongs to the historical heritage of the rich history of Tianjin, as it is one of the first station buildings in China. In order to underline the historical meaning of these relics the urban design concept also refers to these buildings: a second "historic" urban spine is designed whose scale, of course, is smaller than the new elevated spine. By embracing the old buildings a well proportioned square is created whose scale refers to the ancient station. The central axis of the ancient building is prolonged towards the south defining the Front Street of West Railway Station up to the South Channel. Tianjin is a city of ports, a city whose fate and beauty is linked to the sea. Like the busy city of Tianjin the waves are constantly moving, sometimes in a regular row, sometimes big waves reveal the power of the sea. Nothing is more obvious to let the design of the new Tianjin West Railway Station refer to that element which so strongly shapes the history of the city. The large elevated platform above the rail road tracks permits the realizing of a completely new functional layout of the station formerly only known from modern airports. The station is divided into a departure and an arrival terminal positioned at the eastern and western rim of the platform. Instead of separating the arriving and the leaving traveler flow, both needing spacious roads and platforms, the centralized traffic area is shared by both. This results in a very efficient and compressed traffic system which is easy to understand. Thus orientation in the complex system of a station is simplified to a maximum. Former station buildings offer comfort and generous and inviting spaces only to the departing travelers. In opposite to that the arriving guests often leave the station by a small tunnel arriving on a confusing and neglected bus and taxi station. By arriving underneath the gently waved arrival terminal roof of the new Tianjin West Railway Station also those entering this city are offered a warm welcome.

01 Elevation of the wave-form building

Opposite page
Platform area

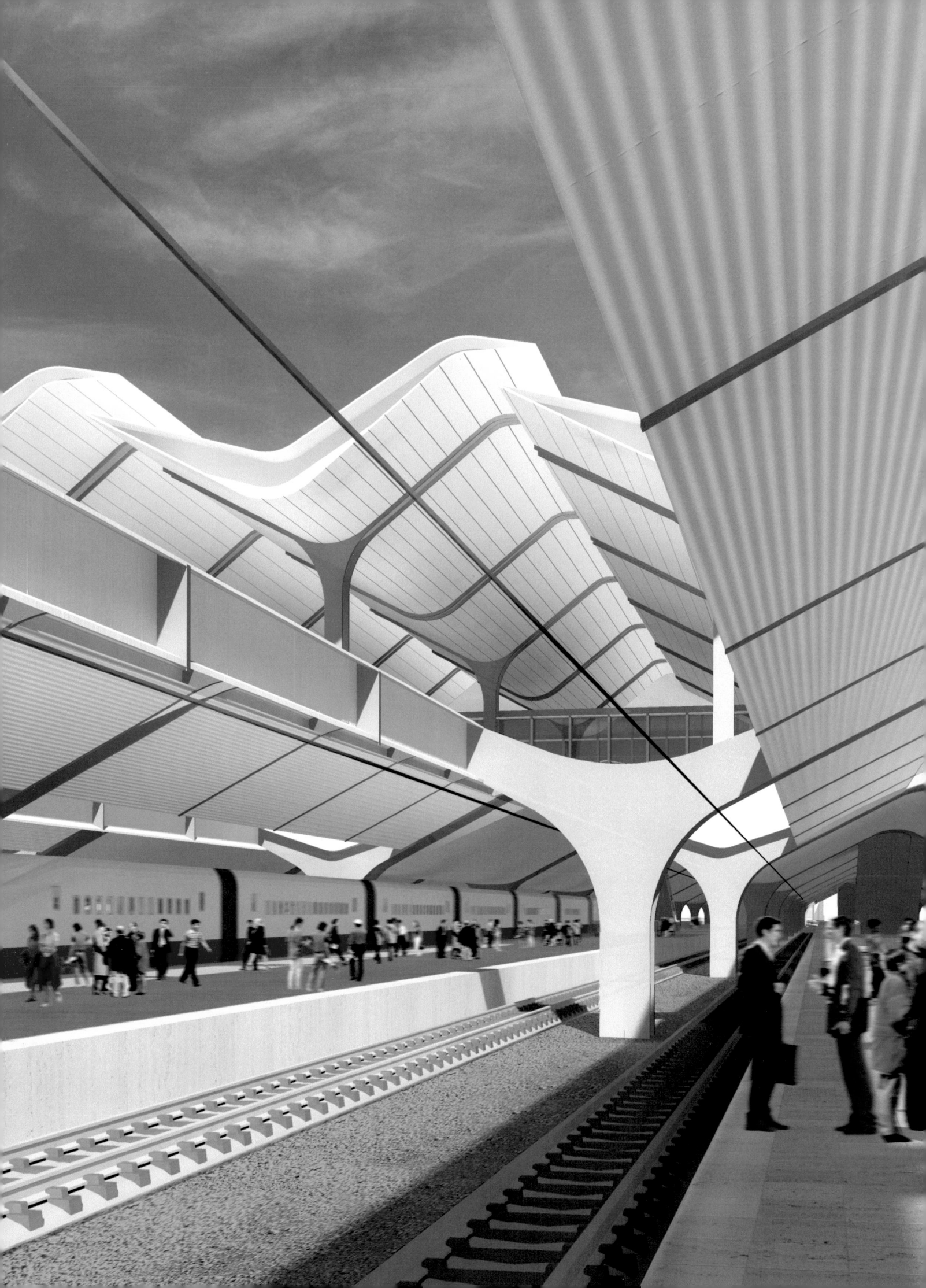

01 The interior appearance
is characterized by the
waved roof.
02 Axonometric projection

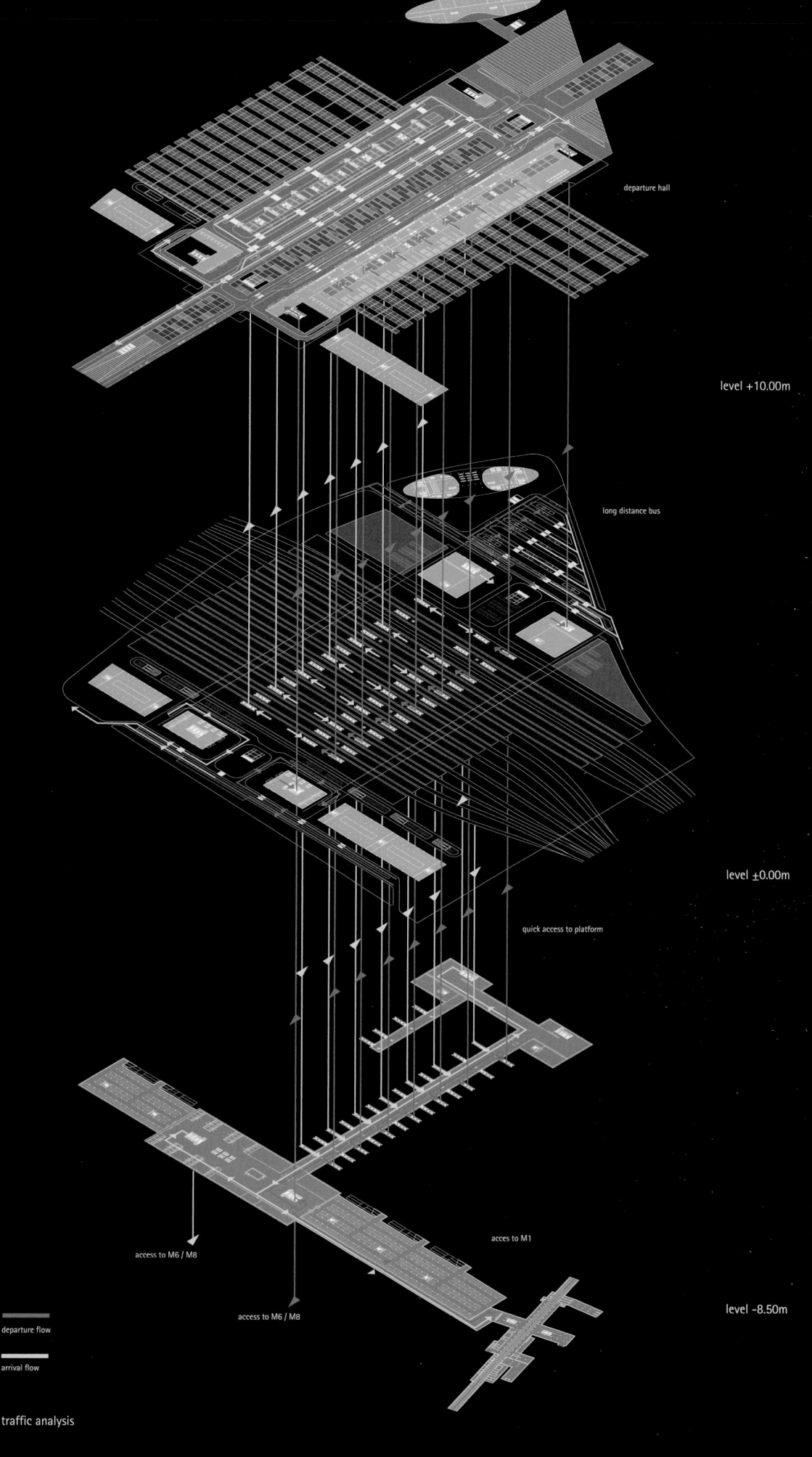

departure hall

level +10.00m

long distance bus

level ±0.00m

quick access to platform

acces to M1

access to M6 / M8

access to M6 / M8

level -8.50m

departure flow

arrival flow

traffic analysis

BAO'AN INTERNATIONAL AIRPORT, TERMINAL 3, SHENZHEN

深圳宝安国际机场T3航站楼

Competition 2007
Design Meinhard von Gerkan
Partner Nikolaus Goetze
Design team Volkmar Sievers, Christian Dahle, Jan Stolte,
Julia Wegner, Deren Akdeniz, Tom Schülke, Markus Carlsen,
Eduard Kaiser, Ingo Beckmann, Nils Dethlefs, Uli Rösler,
Jana Bormann, Kerstin Steinfatt
Client Shenzen Airport (Group) Co., Ltd.
Gross floor area 464,000 m²

Alongside the Hong Kong and Guangzhou airports the Pearl River Delta
will receive its third international air hub with Shenzhen's new airport.
The dominating terminal's overall form is symbolic; its structure is
analogous to the individual elements, aerodynamic shapes and construction principles of an aircraft. The wide-open constructions create
a large and column-free hall. The terminal's character is light and airy,
making the central hall a sheltered yet free area visually open to the
exterior. The building has been designed with forward-looking usage
in mind. The materials and construction elements have been chosen
to be environmentally sustainable. The terminal's energy and material
requirements will be significantly less than those of hitherto existing
construction standards.

01 + Opposite page
The roof lies gently over the building
like a white cloth.
02 Columns and roof supports
are interconnected and merge
harmoniously.

01

02

FAÇADE DESIGN OF HIGH TECH PARK, HEAVY INDUSTRY ZONE, LINGANG

临港产业区高科技园建筑外立面设计

Design Meinhard von Gerkan with Magdalene Weiß, 2005
Partner Nikolaus Goetze
Design and project team Jan Stecher, Wang Yingzhe, Xiangge Peng,
Wang Tao, Shen Na
Client Shanghai Caohejing High Tech Park New Economic Zone
Development Co., Ltd.
Gross floor area 196,000 m²
Construction period 2006–2007

The opening in 2006 of the new deep sea port at Yangshan south of
Shanghai brought rapid development of traffic infrastructure, free port
zones, heavy industry zones and logistics centers to the new city of
Lingang. With its colored façade the new High Tech Park hopes to
symbolize the development potential of Lingang's Heavy Industry Zone.
The simplest building method in China was chosen – concrete skeleton
covered with masonry and plaster. An ostentatious large-format paint
coat in white and deep blue was added as a design feature. Large-
format colored surfaces produce a sense of depth, distance, proximity
as well as strong structural contrasts. Blue and anthracite horizontal
bands on white surfaces create contrasts and clear graphic lines that
in turn create a sense of perspective on the long factory façades.
Where it appears in architecture blue is an explicitly unnatural color.
It is not a material color but rather a deliberate effect. Blue relates to
the color of the sky – in Lingang this is often a hazy gray, but under
favorable wind conditions a radiant blue emerges, streaked with white
clouds and wisps of vapor floating in from the sea.

01

01 Site plan
02 Horizontal color bands give
lightness and floating gracefulness
to the heavy concrete façade.

Opposite page
Blue and anthracite horizontal
bands on white surfaces create
contrasts and clear graphic lines.

Following page
View from the street to the High
Tech Park

02

MANAGEMENT AND SERVICE CENTER OF LINGANG NEW CITY

临港新城行政服务中心

Competition 2004 – 1st prize
Design Meinhard von Gerkan with Magdalene Weiß
Partners Nikolaus Goetze, Wei Wu
Design and project team Jan Stecher, Jörn Ortmann, Xiangge Peng, Yang Li,
Mo Song, Enno Maass, Wang Yingzhe, Wang Yi
Chinese partner practice SIMEE
Client Shanghai Lingang Economic Development Group Co., Ltd.
Gross floor area 45,000 m²
Construction period 2004–2005

An ensemble of buildings consisting of administrative buildings, a bank, a 4-star
hotel, an apartment building and a multifunctional structure accommodating events,
leisure activities and restaurants, forms the new center of the urban neighborhood.
The two juxtaposed buildings housing municipal administration facilities and banks
form the edges of the square on the east side of the site and provide a view of the
plaza from the main access road to the east via the plaza's open side on the west. As
an interconnected group of buildings, the hotel, meeting hall and apartment building
form the conclusion of the square on the west side of the site and face the water
canal to the west, thus taking advantage of its scenic qualities. The buildings
resemble each other in their structure and façade materials – light-colored natural
stone – so as to strengthen the creation of a recognizable city center.
The basic principal of the structures is formed by two intersecting cubes of different
heights, neither of which is more than six stories tall. Thanks to the uniformity of the
building group a clear and recognizable visual element is created on the one hand,
while on the other the differentiation in the detail of the structures' volumes and
façades provides a good sense of proportion and pleasant atmosphere.
The administration building is composed of two structures: the one to the south
faces the square and is five stories high. This structure creates an entry situation
with its 3.90-m-high projecting volume. By means of the pillar and rail glass façade
on the ground floor the entrance appears as a generous, inviting gesture both during
the day and at night. The roof of the projecting volume is designed for use as a
terrace and event area.

01 The conference rooms are
situated above the foyer.
02 Site plan

Opposite page
Detail of the façade with
ventilation flaps

01

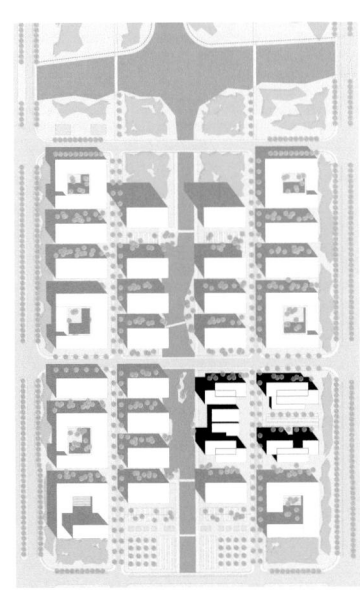

02

TECHNIC CENTER "FREETRADE II", LINGANG

临港国际物流技术中心

Competition 2006 – 1st prize
Design Meinhard von Gerkan
Partner Nikolaus Goetze
Project management Klaus Lenz
Design team Udo Meyer, Matthias Mumm, Eduard Kaiser, Richard Sprenger
Project team Matthias Holtschmidt, Marcus Tanzen, Frederik Heisel, Jens Reichert, Zhu Honghao
Chinese partner practice SIADR, Shanghai Institute of Architectural Design & Research Co., Ltd.
Client Shanghai Lingang International Logistics Development Co., Ltd.
Gross floor area 35,000 m²
Construction period 2006–2007

The concept of the administration building is based on four parallel building structures which are connected via an orthogonally orientated glass passageway. A generous two-story glass entrance hall orientated southwards is the center and the main entrance area of the service complex. The provided dimensions of the building allow for a very flexible subdivision of the office areas: open space offices as well as single offices can be organized. The companies get maximum flexibility for the arrangement of their own office culture. All special areas in the entrance level are directly connected to the outside surroundings and therefore have a direct view on the green and water areas. The office areas that are orientated to the main access area are lifted in parts – by structuring the cubature this way an interesting spatiality comes into being.
The structure is enclosed by a greenish gleaming glass façade with generous room-high glazed parts to bring daylight into the working spaces. The glazed fields, which are all equipped with a window opening for comfort are arranged in a shifted way and thus a vivid impression is created. This theme is repeated on the façades of the two-story-high cubatures which house the special areas. As an interpretation of the main theme the skylights above the main entrance as well as parts of the landscape design are planned checkered.

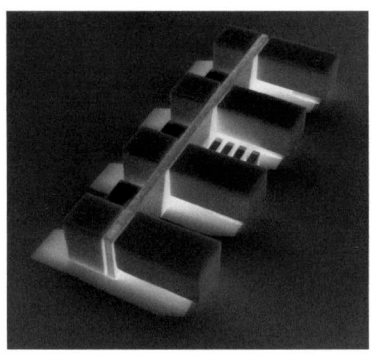

01

01 Model
02 Section

Opposite page
Room-high glass windows afford a maximum of daylight and natural aeration.

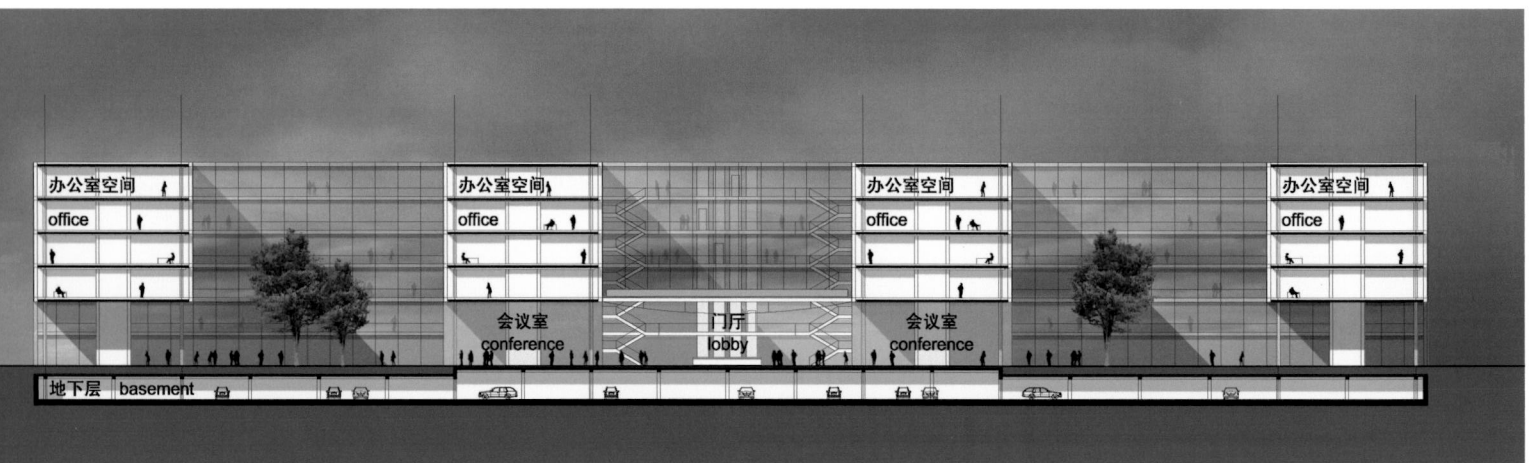

02

01 Main entrance
02 The checkered ceiling
   repeats the façade design
   in the artificial light ...
03 ... and in the daylight.

Following page
Comb structure with main
entrance

02

03

135

CHINA TELECOM, BUILDINGS 12 & 13, SHANGHAI

中国电信上海信息园12号和13号楼

Competition 2005 – 1st prize
Design Meinhard von Gerkan
Partner Nikolaus Goetze
Project management Dirk Heller, Karen Schroeder
Design and project team Meike Schmidt, Friedhelm Chlosta,
Kai Siebke, Christoph Berle, Georg Traun, Holger Schmücker, Di Wu
Chinese partner practice China Information Technology
Designing & Consulting Institute
Client China Telecom Shanghai
Gross floor area 50,000 m²
Construction period 2005–2007

China Telecom Shanghai will concentrate the technical facilities
together with the headquarters, training, research and development
departments in the newly built "China Telecom Information Park". In
2004 gmp won the first prize in an international competition for the
master plan. In cooperation with a local planning institute this idea for
a master plan has been transformed into a legal base for all single
buildings on the site. In 2005 gmp won as well the first prize for plots
B12 & B13 located at the northern end of the landscaped central axis.
Both projects with two buildings and an approximate gross floor area
of 50,000 m² will accommodate technical facilities for digital transfers
as well as administration offices. Vertical positioned glass lamellas
form the outer skin of the buildings. At the B12 building – containing
telecommunication-equipment only – these lamellas are mostly closed,
while at the administration building the lamellas are opened. The
appearance of the glass-lamellas is influenced very much by the
weather conditions. The natural green color – given by the thickness of
the lamellas – is intensified by the grey sky, or changes even to pale
green-grey under the striking sunlight.

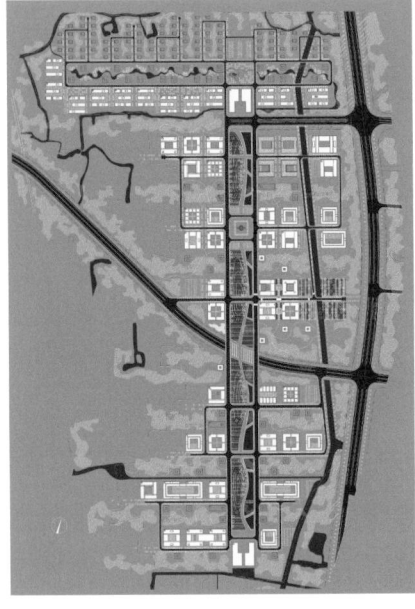

01

02

01 Master plan
02 First stage of construction

Opposite page
Vertically positioned glass
lamellas form the outer skin
of the buildings.

Following page
The reflection emphasizes the
lightness and the translucence
of the envelope of the building.

01

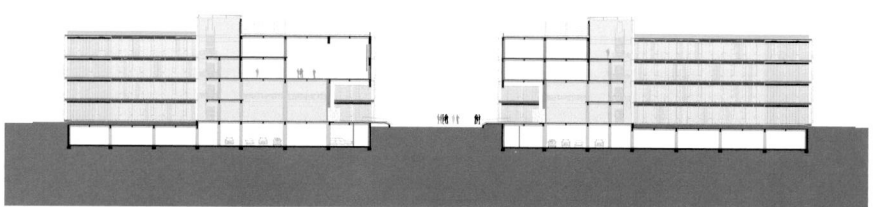

02

01 Inner courtyard with stairwell
02 Section
03 Façade with opened and
closed lamellas

01

01 + 03
Due to the discreet color
design the foyer radiates
calmness and spaciousness.

02 Stairway with inserted
glass banisters

02

03

CHINA TELECOM, BUILDINGS 16A & 16B, SHANGHAI

中国电信上海信息园16a和16b号楼

Competition 2005 – 1st prize
Design Meinhard von Gerkan and Nikolaus Goetze
Project managers Dirk Heller, Karen Schroeder
Project team Christoph Berle, Friedhelm Chlosta, Meike Schmidt,
Holger Schmücker, Kai Siebke, Georg Traun, Katharina Traupe, Di Wu
Chinese partner practice China Information Technology
Designing & Consulting Institute
Client China Telecom Shanghai
Gross floor area 25,000 m²
Construction period 2006–2008

In 2006 gmp won as well the first prize for plots 16a & 16b, located in
the middle of the landscaped central axis. These two square-sized
buildings with a length of 60 m each will accommodate differently
sized lecture halls, conference rooms and administration offices in
Building 16A and a "dormitory" on 5-star-level in Building 16B with
about 300 single rooms and suites on four levels each. The main
entrance foyers face each other at the central drop-off framed by
two glass bridges which connect both buildings at the upper floors.
At the same time the lecture hall building opens to the central axis
with a square-sized courtyard serving as an additional entrance as
well as an "open foyer" for the conference hall. The strong impression
of the buildings is generated by the sandy natural stone clad exterior
of the buildings which contrasts to the carved-out openings filled with
dark-grey glass construction.

01 Preview of the Building 16A

Opposite page
The overall concept of the
"China Telecom Information Park"

01

PUJIANG LOFT COMPLEX FOR MULTIPURPOSE USE, SHANGHAI
上海浦江多功能建筑综合体

Design Meinhard von Gerkan with Magdalene Weiß and
Jan Stecher, 2006
Partner Nikolaus Goetze
Design and project team Viktor Oldiges, Susanne Maijer,
Peng Xiangge, Tan Tian, Zhou Yunkai
Chinese partner practice Shanghai XianDai HuaGai Institute
of Architectural Design & Research Co., Ltd.
Client Shanghai Caohejing Development Area Economic and
Technology Development Co., Ltd.
Gross floor area 145,000 m²
Construction period 2006–2008

The Pujiang development area is located in Shanghai's Pudong area,
closely connected to the center of Shanghai by the Lupu bridge. It
consists of buildings for light industry, office and service use. The
different building types are located around a central plaza together
with a service center which contains a canteen, conference and leisure
spaces. The façades of all buildings are clear plaster-wall façades with
vertical window openings. This common theme unifies all buildings.
At the same time, different variations of the theme – full height
windows, parapets and glass walls – contribute to a large variety.
The landscape concept follows the "Arlington" idea: wide green areas
with single groups of trees form one continuous space. The Grand
Plaza contains a park for recreation. A water pond in front of the
Service Center reflects its façade. Different trees and plants create
a variety of impressions.

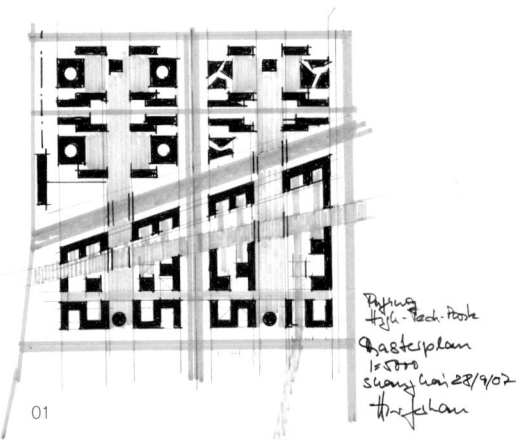

01

01 Sketch
02 The Grand Plaza invites
one to stay and relax.

Opposite page
Clear plaster-wall
façades with vertical
window openings

02

MARRIOTT HOTEL, BINJIANG PLAZA, NINGBO

宁波滨江广场万豪大酒店

01 Site plan
02 The green glass façade gives
the impression of jade.

Opposite page
Ningbo's new landmark

Competition 2004 – 1st prize
Design Meinhard von Gerkan
Partner Nikolaus Goetze
Project manager Volkmar Sievers
Design and project team Simone Nentwig, Matthias Meinheit,
Martina Klostermann, Rouven Oberdiek, Knut Maass, Nicole Loeffler,
Uli Rösler, Evelyn Pasdzierny, Nils Dethlefs, Tilo Günther
Chinese partner practice CJY
Client Ningbo HaiCheng Investment Development Co., Ltd.
Gross floor area 89,600 m²
Construction period 2005–2008

The building project is part of the redevelopment of the western
embankment of the Yuyao River running through the city center of
Ningbo. The 160-m-high tower block protrudes into the Ningbo skyline
and becomes the new landmark of the striving economic region
located south of Shanghai. The building on Heyi Road generates its
form from two curved elements which are connected in their center,
thereby generating the shape of an X. The central axis of the building
is positioned at right angles to the river embankment, thus stating its
relationship to the river. The glazed center accommodates the tower
core with the service functions. A two-storied recess defines the upper
part of the tower. The building accommodates a 5-star Marriott Hotel
with more than 325 rooms; office areas and commercial facilities are
planned along the embankment promenade. The new design of the
landscape park forms part of the planning.

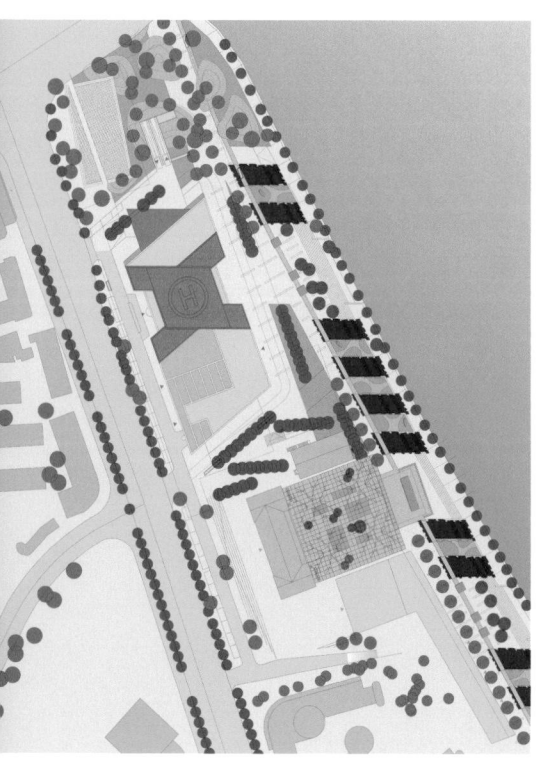

POLY PLAZA, SHOPPING MALL, OFFICE AND APARTMENT COMPLEX, SHANGHAI-PUDONG

上海浦东保利大厦

Competition 2006 – 1st prize
Design Meinhard von Gerkan with Magdalene Weiß
Partners Nikolaus Goetze, Wei Wu
Project managers Alexander Schober, Hao Yan Li,
Annika Schröder
Design team Yi Wang, Eazy Lin, Yingzhe Wang,
Jan Stecher, Jörn Ortmann
Project team Jing Hai Tian, Yu Qi Mao, Jan Blasko,
Chen Fu
Chinese partner practice ECADI
Client Shanghai Poly Xin Real Estate Co., Ltd.
Gross floor area 100,000 m²
Construction period 2007–2009

The Poly Plaza project is situated on the prominent shore of the
HuangPu River near the Lujiazui District. One high-rise tower and four
waterfront buildings with an outer ventilated double façade will provide
office spaces. The site is terraced over three levels, giving direct
basement access through cut-out deep yards leading into the commercial area. The terrace on the second level provides a magnificent
outlook on the riverside. Architecture, green design and light concept
form an aesthetical unity and give a unique aspect to the Shanghai
property market.

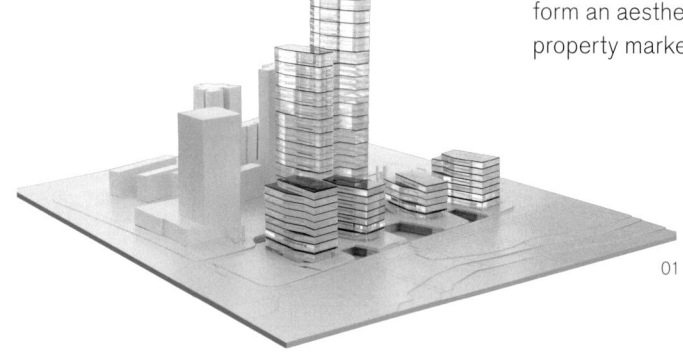

01

01 Model elevation
02 Building site with view over
the HuangPu River
to the skyline of the city

Opposite page
Bird's eye view

02

TWIN TOWERS AND CBD XINGHAI BAY, DALIAN

大连期货广场和星海湾中央商务区

Competition 2003 – 1st prize
Design Meinhard von Gerkan
Partner Nikolaus Goetze
Project managers Karen Schroeder, Dirk Heller
Design and project team Christoph Berle, Friedhelm Chlosta,
Kai Siebke, Holger Schmücker, Sabrina Wilms, Katharina Traupe,
Georg Traun, Meike Schmidt, Markus Carlsen, Eduard Kaiser,
Christian Dahle, Udo Meyer, Wencke Eissing-Poggenberg
Chinese partner practice ECADI
Client Dalian Commodity Exchange
Gross floor area 353,000 m²
Construction periods Tower A: 2004–2008; Tower B: until 2009;
Adjoining building (5-star Howard Johnson Hotel with 300 rooms):
until 2007

The complex is located in the Xinghai District of Dalian at the northern
end of the Xinghai Square, one of the largest squares in China. The Twin
Towers open up to a rectangular public square, which is formed by the
framing buildings in the west and in the east, each composed out of a
horizontally organized building and lower high-rise building at the corners
of the square.
The towers will be mainly used for offices while the ad buildings will be
used as 5-star hotel and SOHO-type lofts and apartments. With 53 floors
above ground the Twin Towers reach an overall height of 242 m on the top
of the helicopter platform. Both towers are based on rectangular floor
plans with about 2,000 m² on each floor. The concrete core within and the
grid-like shell outside are the load-bearing elements. The design of the
façade reflects the structural composition of the building. A white painted
grid of two-story-high V-shaped aluminium profiles forms the primary
structure in front of a dark glass-façade and emphasizes the vertical
direction of the buildings.

01 Building ensemble of the office-towers
and the 5-star hotel in the construction
stage

Opposite page
Future prospects of the Twin Towers

01

OLYMPIC SPORTS CENTER, SHENZHEN

深圳奥林匹克体育中心

01

Competition 2006 – 1st prize
Design Meinhard von Gerkan and Stephan Schütz
with Nicolas Pomränke
Project management Ralf Sieber
Design and project team Ji Xu, Alexander Niederhaus, Cheng Huang, Marlene
Törper, Niklas Veelken, Martin Gänsicke, Stephanie Brendel, Andrea Moritz, Xin
Zheng, Semra Ugur, Kralyu Chobanov, Christian Dorndorf, Lian Kian, Zhou Bin,
Tobias Keyl, Li Ling, Helge Lezius, Xin Meng, Kuno von Haefen, Kathi Mutschlechner
Chinese partner practice SADI, CNADRI, CCDI, BLY
Client "Shenzhen Works Bureau", Bureau of Public Works of Shenzhen Municipality
Site area 870,000 m²
Stadium 60,000 seats
Multifunctional hall 18,000 seats
Swimming hall 3,000 seats
Construction period 2007–2010

The primary elements of the Shenzhen "Olympic Sports Center" are the main sports
stadium, the swimming complex and the multifunctional arena. All three sports
facilities are placed in a clear geometrical order which follows a triangular shape.
Related to the cultural roots the entire complex is designed as a broad landscape
park with all features of a traditional landscape garden: water stretches as well
as plants and trees – this representing motion and development within the garden.
In contrast to this there are elements representing continuity and stability.
They appear as crystalline structures in the form of rocks and stones. The highly
expressive character of the sports venue is reminiscent of giant crystals in a broad
landscape. The dialogue of these expressive objects with the soft shape of the
landscape delivers an unmistakable image to the sports center.

01 1:2 model
02 Detail elevation of the triangular
construction

Opposite page
Overall elevation with main sports
stadium (65,000 seats), multifunctional
arena (18,000 seats) and
swimming complex (3,000 seats)

02

GRAND THEATER, CHONGQING

重庆大剧院

Competition 2003 – 1st prize
Design Meinhard von Gerkan
Partner Nikolaus Goetze
Project manager Volkmar Sievers
Design team Heiko Thiess, Monika van Vught, Robert Friedrichs,
Matthias Ismael, Tobias Jortzick, Dominik Reh, Christian Dahle,
Julia Gronbach
Project team Knut Maass, Huan Zhu, Kerstin Steinfatt, Jan Stolte,
Nils Dethlefs
Chinese partner practice ECADI
Client Chongqing Urban Construction Investment
Gross floor area 100,000 m²
Construction period 2005–2009

With its close proximity to the water, the "Grand Theater" seems to hover
above the Yangtse River. A stone platform base supports the glass
sculpture; the ground plan and elevation are subject to strict functional
requirements despite their seemingly arbitrary expressiveness and
maritime analogy. Two concert halls with their respective foyers are
situated in the longitudinal axis, similar to the "keel line" of a ship, thus
forming entrance areas at the bow and the stern. In the center, in other
words "midship" of these entrance areas, is the exhibition hall which joins
the theater foyers together.

01 Sketch
02 Structural construction
detail in 2007
03 Longitudinal section

Opposite page
Top view and side view
produce the metaphoric
portrayal of a ship as a
floating theater building
in a sea of light.

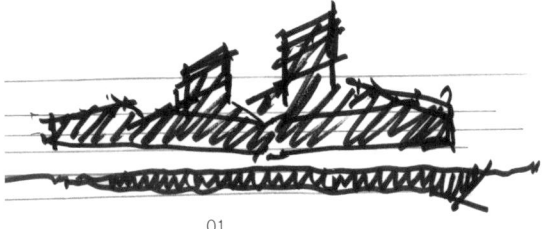

01

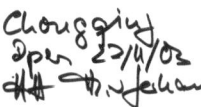

02

03

GRAND THEATER, QINGDAO

青岛大剧院

Competition 2004 – 1st prize
Design Meinhard von Gerkan and Stephan Schütz with Nicolas Pomränke
Design and project team Clemens Kampermann, Johannes Erdmann, Kian Lian, Gerd Meyer, Chongsong Dong, Li Ling, Annette Löber, Xin Meng, Jochen Sültrup, Sophie von Mansberg
Chinese partner practice ECADI
Client Qingdao Conson Industrial Corporation
Gross floor area 80,000 m²
Opera hall 1,600 seats
Concert hall 1,200 seats
Multifunctional hall 400 seats
Construction period 2005–2008

With its highest peak rising 1,134 m above the sea level the mount Laoshan and the surrounding peaks are situated in the southeastern Shandong peninsula. Due to the unique climatic situation the Laoshan Mountains are very often wrapped in clouds which lend a particularly mystic atmosphere to the scenery. Mountains and clouds: the aim of the design is to transform landscape and the power of nature into architectural language. Like a mountain plateau an open terrace rises up from the park and forms a generous public square which is orientated to the sea in the southwest and to the mountains in the northeast. The terrace forms an open space underneath the floating clouds like a roof. By raising the plateau 4.5 m and turning it slightly to the sea and to the Laoshan Mountains a clear visual relation to the most scenic spots of Laoshan is produced. From the platform the major functions of the Grand Theater grow up like rocks of granite, which is the local stone: 1. the opera house in the north, 2. the concert and multifunctional hall in the south, 3. the media center in the west, 4. the Artist Reception and Training Center in the east. Analogous to the predominant weather situation in the Laoshan Mountains the roof of the Grand Theater appears like a cloud drifting along the mountain like volumes of singular buildings. In this way a most poetic architectural image is created which makes the buildings recognizable all over the world. The expressive and massive rocks of the architectural landscape and the light and elegant cloud-like roof form an exciting architectural dialogue.

01 Future concert and multifunctional hall as rendering …
02 … and as building site

Opposite page
Bird's eye view of the building ensemble

01

02

MARITIME MUSEUM, LINGANG NEW CITY

临港新城国家航海博物馆

Consultancy 2005
Design Meinhard von Gerkan
Partner Nikolaus Goetze
Project managers Klaus Lenz, Marcus Tanzen
Design and project team Richard Sprenger, Eazy Lin, Jens Reichert,
Birgit Föllmer, Udo Meyer, Elena Melnikova, Ben Grope,
Markus Carlsen
Chinese partner practice SIADR
Client Shanghai Harbour City Investment Co.
Gross floor area 72,400 m²
Construction period 2006–2008

The solitaire-type structures of the Maritime Museum, the Youth
Center and the Library are combined to form a homogenous overall
complex with the help of the uniform use of shapes and materials.
Centrally placed between the Library and the Youth Center, the
Maritime Museum with its expressive roof shape stands out distinctly
and independently against this formal overall construction. Two light
roof shells, facing each other and overlapping, that in the broadest
sense evoke in the observer the idea of a maritime shape and an
analogy to a "sail", create the identity-forming landmark of the Museum
that is so decisive for the overall character of the complex. The large,
hall-like space below this roof construction is intended for the exhibition of large ancient ships that have been assessed as being valuable
to cultural history. The entwined "sails" stand freely on a pedestal in
which all the functions of the Museum are accommodated. Spacious
open staircases are inviting places to linger and bear an immediate
relation to the landscaped open spaces. The formal design elements of
the publicly accessible pedestal that can be reached via a generously
arranged outside staircase can also be found in the two directly
neighboring buildings, the Library and the Youth Center.

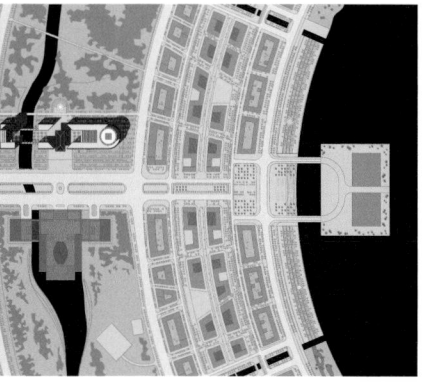

01

01 Site plan
02 Model
03 Construction state in 2007
with built watercourses

Opposite page
Exhibition hall under the "sail"
with ancient ship

02

03

SHANGHAI NANHUI DISTRICT ADMINISTRATIVE OFFICE CENTER, LINGANG NEW CITY

临港新城上海南汇区行政办公中心

Competition 2005 – 1st prize
Design Meinhard von Gerkan
Partner Nikolaus Goetze
Project management Jörn Ortmann
Design team Li Yang, Mo Song, Xiange Peng, Yanli Hao, Chen Fu, Evelyn Pasdzierny, Alexandra Kühne, Barbara Henke
Chinese partner practice SIADR
Client Government of the Nanhui District
Gross floor area 100,860 m²
Construction period 2006–2008

The exposed position of the plot by one of the main access roads of Lingang New City demands a similarly exposed as well as distinct architectural composition of the individual main buildings and annexes of the Office Center which will be grouped together to form a superordinate ensemble. The central square in the complex is spanned by a large quadratic roof; a curtain of water permanently running down from this lends additional emphasis to the square and ensures pleasant cooling and a high incentive to linger here. In the east and west of the complex two light-filled entrance halls covered with shed roofs adjoin this patio. In the main building on the east side a cascade-like staircase leads to the central zone which is crowned by a conference hall with capacity for up to 2,500 people. On the western side of the complex the annexes are grouped around the inner courtyard with its trees and the river flowing through it.

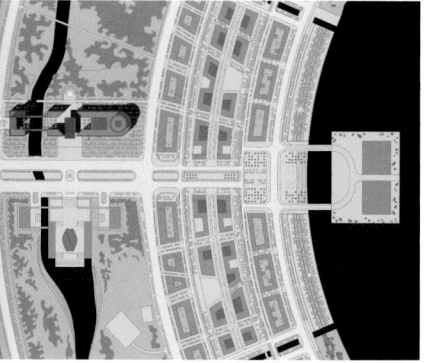

01

01 Site plan
02 Courtyard with foyer

Opposite page
View from the top of the high-rise building across the courtyard and the conference hall to the lake of Lingang New City

02

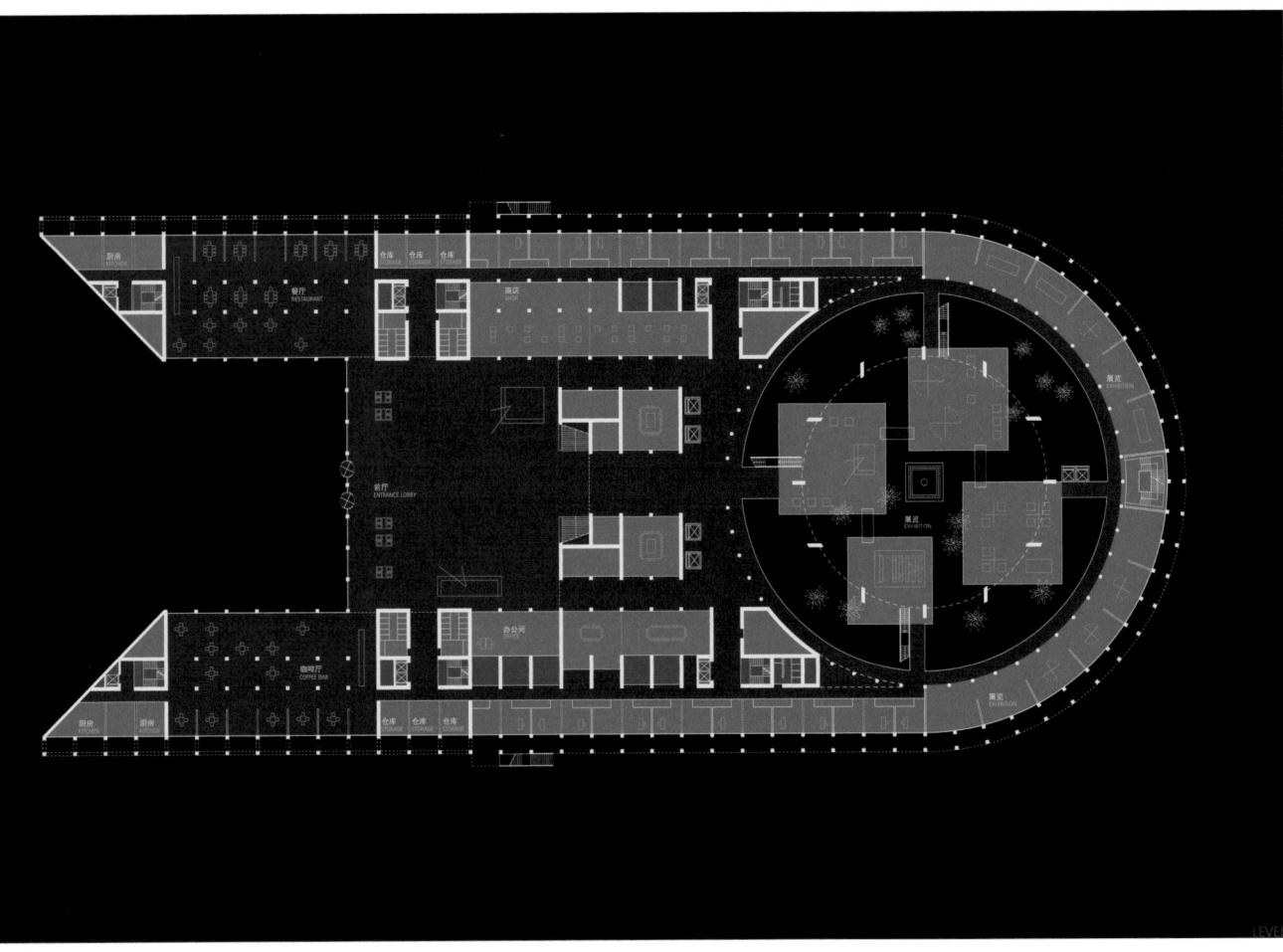

01

02

03

04

01 Plan
02 Section

Building complex elevation as
03 Rendering
04 Building site

PARK LIGHTS, LINGANG NEW CITY

临港新城城市照明

01 Lighting concept
02 + Opposite
First impressions of the promenade's
new illumination

Design Meinhard von Gerkan with Magdalene Weiß and
Yingzhe Wang, 2005
Chinese partner practice Zumtobel China
Client Shanghai Harbour City Development (Group) Co., Ltd.
Construction period 2005

Four-armed lights flank the shore promenade of the central
round lake in Lingang New City. Each cross stele is made up of
four steel T-squares, which clamp the brackets in the four axes
laterally. The four bodies of light at the end of the brackets are
made of frosted glass cylinders. As points of light, they are
reflected in the water and are visible across the lake. At the
same time the integrated and vertical down lights provide the
necessary illumination for the benches and pedestrian paths.
The series of lights lends proportion and detail to the area,
creating an atmospheric lighting scenario for pedestrians
walking along the curved water edge, as well as a foreground
for the urban promenade from afar.

01

02

CHRONOLOGY

German School and Apartment House in Beijing
Competition 1998, 1st prize
Design Meinhard von Gerkan with Michael Biwer
Partner Klaus Staratzke
Project managers Michael Biwer, Sibylle Kramer
Design team Bettina Groß, Elke Hoffmeister
Project team Michèle Watenphul, Knut Maass, Ulrich Rösler, Diana Heinrich, Jörn Bohlmann, Rüdiger von Helmolt, Robert Wildegger
Structural engineers Weber-Poll Ingenieure
Operating construction company Philipp Holzmann
Client Fed. Rep. of Germany
Gross floor area School 9,658 m², Apartment House 9,657 m²
Construction period 1999–2000

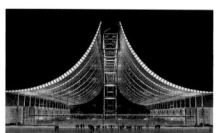

Trade Fair, Shanghai-Pudong
Competition 1998
Design Volkwin Marg
Design team Eun Young Yi, Gunter Köhnlein, Erik Recke, Wolfram Grothe, Marc Frohn, Mario Rojas Toledo, Thomas Behr
Gross floor area 236,000 m²

International Convention & Exhibition Center, Nanning
Competition 1999, 1st prize
Design Meinhard von Gerkan and Nikolaus Goetze
Project managers Dirk Heller, Karen Schroeder
Design team Oliver Christ, Andreas Gärtner, Mike Berrier, Jens Niemann, Antonio Caetita-Soeiro, Malte Wolf
Project team Christoph Berle, Kai Siebke, Georg Traun, Friedhelm Chlosta, Meike Schmidt, Wencke Eissing, Oliver Christ, Stefanie Schupp, Jochen Schwarz, Eckhard Send, Iris van Hülst, Thomas Eberhardt
Chinese partner practice Guangxi Architectural Comprehensive Design & Research Institute
Structural engineers Schlaich, Bergermann and Partners
Technical building equipment HL-Technik, Hamburg
Landscape architects Breimann & Bruun, Hamburg
Client Nanning International Convention & Exhibition Co., Ltd.

Gross floor area ca. 165,000 m²
Construction period 1999–2003/2005

International Convention & Exhibition Center, Guangzhou
Competition 2000, 2nd prize
Design Volkwin Marg with Marc Ziemons
Partner Nikolaus Goetze
Design team Thomas Schuster, Sven Greiser, Tom Eberhard, Gudrun von Schau, Kristina Milani, Martin Marschner, Moritz Hoffmann-Becking, Mario Rojas-Toledo
Client Guangzhou Urban Planning Office
Gross floor area 520,000 m²

Tourism Center, Hangzhou
Competition 2000, 1st prize
Design Meinhard von Gerkan
Partner Nikolaus Goetze
Project manager Volkmar Sievers
Design team, phase 1 Walter Gebhardt, Christoph Berle, Andreas Gärtner, Astrid Lapp, Jochen Meyer
Design team, phase 2 Christoph Berle, Wu Wei, Justus Klement, Tanja Markovic, Kristina Milani, Andrea Moritz
Project team, phase 1 Heiner Gietmann, Dirk Hünerbein, Dominik Reh, Holger Schmücker
Project team, phase 2 Simone Nentwig, Jörn Bohlmann, Karen Heckel, Nicole Loeffler, Rouven Oberdiek, Thies Böke, Tobias Plinke, Andrea Moritz, Heike Kugele, Nils Dethlefs, Leif Henning
Chinese partner practice ZADRI, Zhejiang Building Design & Research Institute, Hangzhou
Client Hangzhou Canhigh Estate Co.
Gross floor area 117,000 m²
Construction period 2004–2008

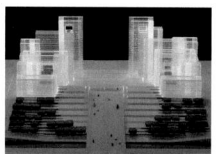

G.W. Plaza, Beijing
Competition 2000, 1st prize
Design Meinhard von Gerkan
Design team Kristian Uthe-Spencker, Stephan Schütz, Tim Schmitt, Markus Pfisterer
Client G.W. Group Ltd., Beijing

World Exhibition and Sports Center, Beijing
Competition 2000, commended
Design Meinhard von Gerkan and Joachim Zais

Design team Christoph Berle, Astrid Lapp, Jens Niemann, Matias Otto, Hajo Paap, Magdalene Weiß, Monika van Vught, Ioannis Zonitsas
Client Beijing Planning Committee
Gross floor area 3,410,000 m²

Cultural Forum, Lang Fang near Beijing
Consultancy 2000
Design Meinhard von Gerkan
Partner Nikolaus Goetze
Design team Jessica Weber, Heiko Thiess, Annika Schröder, Sona Kazemi, Stephanie Heß, Richard Sprenger, Kristina Milani, Christoph Berle, Philipp Kamps, Justus Klement
Client Lang Fang Urban Planning Bureau
Area 44 ha

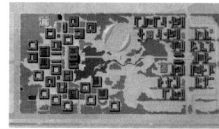

New Campus of the Shenyang Architectural and Civil Engineering Institute
Competition 2000, 2nd prize
Design Meinhard von Gerkan and Joachim Zais
Design team Astrid Lapp, Jochen Meyer, Sigrid Müller, Jörn Ortmann, Matias Otto, Monika van Vught, Claudia Weitemeier, Gabi Wysocki, Ioannis Zonitsas

Qingdao Liuting Airport
Competition 2000
Design Meinhard von Gerkan with Walter Gebhardt
Design team Stefanie Driessen, Andreas Gärtner, Jens Niemann, Rüdiger von Helmolt, Patrick Huhn, Thomas Pehlke
In cooperation with Agiplan and Initec
Client Qingdao Airport Construction Headquarters

Xinzhao Residential Area, Beijing
Design Meinhard von Gerkan and Nikolaus Goetze, 2000
Project managers Dirk Heller, Karen Schroeder
Design and project team Christoph Berle, Kai Siebke, Friedhelm Chlosta, Georg Traun, Meike Schmidt, Wencke Eissing-Poggenberg, Holger Wermers, Oliver Christ
Chinese partner practice Beijing Victory Star Architecture Design Co., Beijing Huazi Engineering Design Co.
Client Beijing Xinzhao Real Development Co., Beijing Town-Country Houses Construction Development Co.

Gross floor area of 1st and 2nd phase 235,000 m² – 2,163 apartments
Construction period of 1st and 2nd phase 2001–2004

Exhibition Pavilion for Xinzhao Residential Area, Beijing
Design Meinhard von Gerkan, 2000
Project manager Dirk Heller
Design and project team Christoph Berle, Astrid Lapp
Client Beijing Xinzhao Real Development Co., Beijing Town-Country Houses Construction Development Co.
Gross floor area 1,400 m²
Construction period 2000–2001

Convention & Exhibition Center, Shenzhen
Competition 2001, 1st prize
Design Volkwin Marg and Nikolaus Goetze
Project managers Marc Ziemons, Thomas Schuster
Design and project team Carsten Plog, Katja Zoschke, Susanne Winter, Dirk Balser, Sven Greiser, Martin Marschner, Moritz Hoffmann-Becking, Wei Wu, Martina Klostermann, Iris van Hülst, Flori Wagner, Tina Stahnke, Marina Hoffmann, Karen Seekamp, Heike Kugele, Otto Dorn, Jeanny Rieger
Structural engineers, design Schlaich, Bergermann and Partners
Technical building equipment, design HL-Technik
Landscape architects, design Breimann & Bruun
Light planning Schlotfeldt Licht
Chinese partner practice China Northeast Architectural Design Institute, Shenzhen
Client Shenzhen Convention & Exhibition Center
Gross floor area 256,000 m²
Construction period 2002–2005

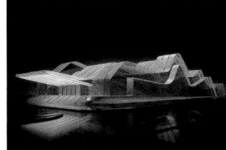

Oriental Art Center, Shanghai
Exhibition complex
Competition 2001, 1st prize
Design Meinhard von Gerkan with Walter Gebhardt
Partner Joachim Zais
Design team Evelyn Pasdzierny, Jörn Bohlmann, Yingdi Wang, Tilo Günther, Barbara Henke, Rouven Oberdiek
Client Pudong Municipal Culture Radio & TV Administration, Shanghai
Gross floor area 44,000 m²

Mobile Communication Center, Guangzhou
Competition 2001, 2nd prize
Design Meinhard von Gerkan
Partner Nikolaus Goetze
Design team Volkmar Sievers, Simone Nentwig, Tobias Plinke, Rouven Oberdiek
Client Guangdong Mobile Communication Co.
Gross floor area 16,640 m²

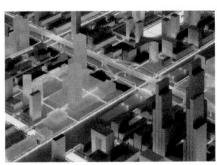

Central Business District, Beijing
Competition 2001
Design Meinhard von Gerkan and Nikolaus Goetze
Design team Jessica Weber, Heiko Thiess, Martin Tamke, Michael Bucherer, Nico Rickert
Proprietor Construction & Management Office of Beijing CBD
Area 4,000 m²

Fortune Plaza, Beijing
Competition 2001, 1st prize
Design Meinhard von Gerkan with Stephan Schütz and Kristian Uthe-Spencker
Design team Christian Dorndorf, Nicolas Pomränke, Sophie von Mansberg
Client Beijing Xiangjiang Real Estate Development Co., Ltd.
Gross floor area 700,000 m²

Finance Street, Beijing
Competition 2001, 3rd prize
Design Meinhard von Gerkan and Klaus Staratzke
Design team Michael Biwer, Hinrich Müller, Udo Meyer, Christoph Schulze-Kölln, Julia Strunk, Tobias Plinke, Melanie Klusmeier, Barbara Henke, Myriam Engels, Bettina Groß
Client Beijing Finance Street Construction & Development Co., Ltd.

New City Jia Ding
Urban planning
Consultancy 2001
Design Meinhard von Gerkan
Design team Hinrich Müller, Heiko Thiess, Jessica Weber, Svenia Oehmig, Julia Strunk, Holger Schmücker
Client Jia Ding Urban Planning Administration
Gross floor area 2,262,000 m²

Shanghai South Railway Station
Competition 2001
Design Meinhard von Gerkan
Design team Walter Gebhardt, Evelyn Pasdzierny, Simone Nentwig, Jörn Bohlmann, Lars Neininger, Christoph Thomsen

Client Construction Command Post of Shanghai South Railway Station of Shanghai Railway Administration
Gross floor area 60,000 m²

International Convention, Exhibition and Sports Center, Harbin
Competition 2001
Design Volkwin Marg
Design team Marek Nowak, Stefan Nixdorf, Christoph Helbich, Stephan Menke, Sven Laurin, Johannes Klein, Burkhard Floors
Client Harbin International Conference Exhibition Center Company Ltd.
Gross floor area 230,000 m²

Shih Chien University Gymnasium, Taipei, Taiwan
Design Meinhard von Gerkan with Monika van Vught, 2001/2002
Partner Joachim Zais
Design team Udo Meyer, Claudia Schultz, Friedhelm Chlosta
Client Shih Chien University
Gross floor area 20,000 m²

Development Central Building, Guangzhou
Competition 2001, 1st prize
Design Meinhard von Gerkan and Nikolaus Goetze with Volkmar Sievers
Design and project team Simone Nentwig, Huan Zhu, Jörn Bohlmann, Robert Wildegger, Tilo Günther, Lars Neininger, Andrea Moritz, Tobias Plinke, Heike Kugele, Nils Dethlefs, Knut Maass
Structural engineers Ove Arup & Partners
Chinese partner practice GZDI, Guangzhou Design Institute
Client Guangzhou Developing New City Investment Co., Ltd.
Gross floor area 78,600 m²
Height 150 m
Floors 37
Construction period 2002–2005

Yuelu Campus Town, Changsha
Competition 2001, 1st prize
Design Meinhard von Gerkan
Partner Joachim Zais
Design team Dominik Reh, Jörn Herrmann, Udo Meyer, Gabi Wysocki, Xialong Hu, Huan Zhu
Client Human Provincial Development Planning Commission
Gross floor area 2,872,500 m²

Pacific City, Beijing
Urban planning
Competition 2001
Design Meinhard von Gerkan
Partner Nikolaus Goetze
Design team Karen
Schroeder, Dirk Heller, Oliver
Christ, Wencke Eissing, Svenia
Oehmig, Ole Seidel
Client World Lexus Pacific
Ltd. Beijing
Gross floor area
450,000 m²

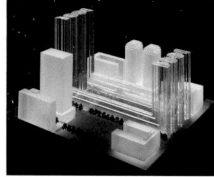

CATIC Zone, Shenzhen
Urban planning
Competition 2001, 1st prize
Design Meinhard von Gerkan
with Walter Gebhardt
Project team Evelyn
Pasdzierny, Heiner Gietmann,
Mark Kelting, Rouven
Oberdiek, Barbara Henke,
Matthias Meinheit
Client Shenzhen Catic Real
Estate Inc.
Gross floor area
280,000 m²

**Shenyang Hunnan New
District**
Competition 2001,
2nd prize group
Design Meinhard von Gerkan
Design team Stephan Schütz,
Kristian Uthe-Spencker,
Christian Dorndorf, Michèle
Rüegg, Katina Roloff

**East China Normal
University,
Jia Ding Campus**
Competition 2001
Design Meinhard von Gerkan
with Walter Gebhardt
Design team Hinrich Müller,
Sigrid Müller, Heiko Thiess,
Matias Otto, Gunnar Müller,
Matthias Meinheit, Sven Gaedt,
Georg Traun
Client East China Normal
University
Gross floor area
200,000 m²

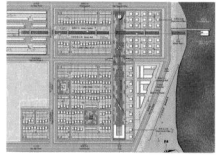

Mapo Villas, Beijing
Consultancy 2001
Design Meinhard von Gerkan
and Nikolaus Goetze
Design team Oliver Christ,
Karen Seekamp, Dirk Balser,
Katja Zoschke, Iris van Hülst
Client Beijing Town-Country
Houses Construction
Development Co.
Gross floor area
600,000 m²

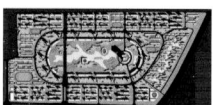

Ziwei Garden City, Xi'an
Competition 2002
Design Meinhard von Gerkan
Design team Stephan Schütz,
Doris Schäffler, Giuseppina
Orto, Gregor Hoheisel
Client XAGK Group
Area 147 ha

**Zhongguancun Cultural
Center, Beijing**
Competition 2002, 1st prize
Design Meinhard von Gerkan
Partner Stephan Schütz
Project manager Nicolas
Pomränke
Design and project team
Doris Schäffler, Gero Heimann,
Xia Lin, Giuseppina Orto, Jan
Pavuk, Margret Böthig
Structural engineers
Schlaich, Bergermann and
Partners
Chinese partner practice
Sunlight Architects &
Engineers Co., Ltd.
Client China Zhongguancun
Culture Development Co., Ltd.
Gross floor area 85,000 m²
Height 80 m
Floors 17
Construction period
2003–2006

**Jiahe Office- and
Commercial Building,
Ningbo**
Design Meinhard von Gerkan
with Volkmar Sievers, 2002
Partner Nikolaus Goetze
Design and project team
Simone Nentwig, Huan Zhu,
Jörn Bohlmann, Nicole
Loeffler, Tilo Günther
Client Hangzhou Canhigh
Estate Co.
Gross floor area
215,000 m²
Construction period
2004–2008

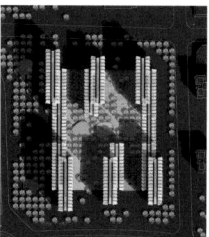

Chaoyang Plaza, Beijing
Urban planning
Competition 2002
Design Meinhard von Gerkan
Design team Stephan Schütz,
Nicolas Pomränke
Client Beijing Unionland
Property Development Co., Ltd.
Gross floor area
400,000 m²

**New Town Anting –
Development
of a German Town**
Competition 2002
Design Meinhard von Gerkan
with Stephan Schütz
Project managers Stephan
Schütz, Doris Schäffler
Project team Giuseppina
Orto, Gero Heimann
Structural engineers The
Ninth Design and Research
Institute, Shanghai
Client Shanghai International
Automobile City Real Estate
Co., Ltd.
Area 100,000 m²

New Town Anting – Church
Design Meinhard von Gerkan
with Stephan Schütz, 2002
Project team Giuseppina
Orto, Gero Heimann

Gross floor area 3,400 m²
Construction period
2006–2007

**New Town Anting – Theater
and Boarding House**
Design Meinhard von Gerkan
with Stephan Schütz, 2002
Project team Giuseppina
Orto, David Schenke,
Lan Chen, Chunsong Dong
Gross floor area 20,500 m²
Construction period
2006–2007

**New Town Anting –
Shopping Mall**
Design Meinhard von Gerkan
with Stephan Schütz, 2002
Project team
David Schenke, Chunsong
Dong, Jing Jun Zhou
Gross floor area 41,100 m²
Construction period
2006–2007

**Museum and Archive,
Shanghai-Pudong**
Competition 2002, 1st prize
Design Meinhard von Gerkan
Partner Nikolaus Goetze
Project managers Dirk
Heller, Karen Schroeder
Design and project team
Christoph Berle, Georg Traun,
Friedhelm Chlosta, Kai Siebke,
Meike Schmidt, Wencke
Eissing-Poggenberg, Wei Wu,
Holger Wermers, Birgit
Föllmer, Hinrich Müller, Udo
Meyer, Thomas Eberhardt
Chinese partner practice
SIADR, Shanghai Institute of
Architectural Design &
Research Co., Ltd.
Client City of Shanghai, New
District Pudong
Gross floor area 41,000 m²
Construction period
2003–2006

CCTV Beijing
Office and commercial
block with TV studios
Competition 2002
Design Meinhard von Gerkan
with Doris Schäffler and
Stephan Schütz
Design team Giuseppina
Orto, Nicolas Pomränke, David
Schenke, Gregor Hoheisel,
Patrick Pfleiderer
Client CCTV Beijing
Gross floor area
551,000 m²

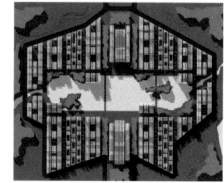

**Songjiang University for
Visual Arts, Shanghai**
Competition 2002
Design Meinhard von Gerkan
Design team Doris Schäffler,
Giuseppina Orto, Stephan
Schütz, Nicolas Pomränke
Client Administration Bureau
of Songjiang University
Gross floor area
120,000 m²

Hotel and Commercial Block, Hubin, Hangzhou
Competition 2002
Design Meinhard von Gerkan
Partner Nikolaus Goetze
Design team Volkmar Sievers, Andrea Moritz, Jörn Bohlmann, Simone Nentwig, Huan Zhu, Thies Böke, Nicole Loeffler, Tobias Plinke, Rouven Oberdiek
Gross floor area 150,000 m²

Campus Town, Nanjing-Xianling
Competition 2002
Design Meinhard von Gerkan
Design team Walter Gebhardt, Annika Schröder, Evelyn Pasdzierny, Eduard Kaiser, Hinrich Müller, Christian Krüger
Client Urban City Planning Administration of Nanjing
Gross floor area 1,400,000 m²

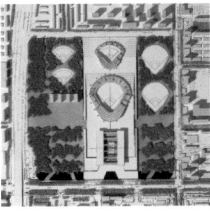

Wukesong Cultural and Sports Center, Beijing
Competition 2002
Design Meinhard von Gerkan
Partner Jürgen Hillmer
Design team Mike Berrier, Tanja Gutena, Hauke Petersen, Markus Carlsen, Heiko Thiess, Jörn Herrmann
Client Beijing Municipal Planning Commission
Area 50 ha

Century City, Beijing
Urban planning
Competition 2002
Design Meinhard von Gerkan with Stephan Schütz and Nicolas Pomränke
Design team Doris Schäffler, Giuseppina Orto, David Schenke, Gero Heimann, Chunsong Dong
Client Beijing Century City Real Estate Development Co., Ltd.
Gross floor area 463,000 m²

Beijing Olympic Green Master plan for the Olympic Games 2008
Competition 2002
Design Meinhard von Gerkan
Partner Joachim Zais
Design team Sigrid Müller, Dominik Reh, Julia Künzer, Friedhelm Chlosta, Hung-Wei Hsu
Client City of Beijing
Gross floor area 2,160,000 m²

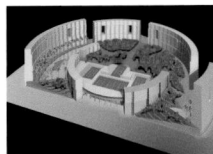

Residential Area with Tennis Center, Shenzhen
Competition 2002
Design Meinhard von Gerkan with Walter Gebhardt

Design team Evelyn Pasdzierny, Matthias Ismael, Enno Maass, Matthias Meinheit, Hans Münchhalfen, Jan Stecher
Client Jin Di Group Co., Ltd. Golden Field Group Co., Ltd.
Gross floor area 250,000 m²

Chaoyang Park, Beijing
Urban planning
Competition 2002
Design Meinhard von Gerkan
Design team Thomas Krautwald, Peter Glaser, Michael Bucherer, Peter Tröster, Tillmann Weiß, Birgit Wachhorst
Client Beijing Gouxing Real Estate Development Co., Ltd.
Gross floor area 500,000 m²

Anti-Aging Clinic near Beijing
Design Meinhard von Gerkan, 2002
Design team Doris Schäffler, Kristian Uthe-Spencker, Katina Roloff, Christiane Scheuermann
Gross floor area 6,000 m²

Jian Gou Dong, Shanghai
Urban planning
Design Meinhard von Gerkan, 2002
Partner Nikolaus Goetze
Design team Udo Meyer, Niko Rickert, Beate Quaschning, Michèle Watenphul, Evagelia Segkis
Client Shanghai COB Development Co., Ltd.
Gross floor area 448,000 m²

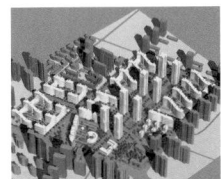

Duftberg Villas, Beijing
Consultancy 2002
Design Meinhard von Gerkan with Klaus Lenz
Design team Monika van Vught, Jörn Ortmann, Hauke Petersen
Gross floor area 81,000 m²

Residential Area, Tianjin
Design Meinhard von Gerkan, 2002
Partner Nikolaus Goetze
Design team Dirk Heller, Karen Schroeder, Meike Schmidt, Friedhelm Chlosta, Christoph Berle, Wencke Eissing, Georg Traun, Kai Siebke, Holger Wermers
Client Beijing Yin Xin Guang Hua Real Estate Development PTY Ltd.
Gross floor area 730,000 m²

Tsinghua University, Academy of Arts and Design, Beijing
Competition 2002, one 1st prize
Design Meinhard von Gerkan
Design team Doris Schäffler, Stephan Schütz, Giuseppina Orto, Nicolas Pomränke, Gero Heimann
Client Tsinghua University Beijing
Gross floor area 80,000 m²

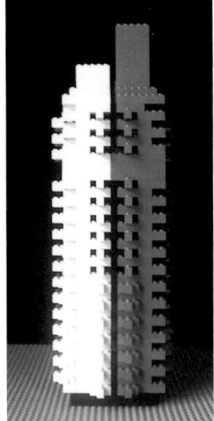

Jingan International District, Shanghai
Competition 2002
Design Meinhard von Gerkan
Partner Nikolaus Goetze
Design team Annika Schröder, Heiko Thiess, Jörn Herrmann, Hun-Wei Hsu, Stephanie Heß, Eduard Kaiser, Albrecht Bauer
Client Urban Planning Administration of Jingan District, Shanghai; Fine Time Investments Co., Ltd., Hong Kong
Gross floor area 862,400 m²

Yangshan New City
Competition 2002
Design Meinhard von Gerkan
Partner Klaus Staratzke
Design team Sigrid Müller, Annika Schröder, Hung-Wei Hsu, Eduard Kaiser, Stephanie Heß
Client Urban Planning Society of China and Development and Environment Protection Bureau of Shengsi County
Gross floor area 2,100,000 m²

CaiYuan Building, Beijing
Competition 2002
Design Meinhard von Gerkan
Design team Evelyn Pasdzierny, Matthias Ismael, Matthias Meinheit, Niko Rickert, Barbara Henke, Rouven Oberdiek
Client Beijing Jianji Tianrun Estate Co., Ltd.
Gross floor area 180,000 m²

Office Building, Beijing
Competition 2002
Design Meinhard von Gerkan
Design team Volkmar Sievers, Simone Nentwig, Huan Zhu, Nicole Loeffler, Tilo Günther, Rouven Oberdiek
Gross floor area 90,000 m²

Residential Area "Sunshine 100", Chongqing
Consultancy 2002
Design Meinhard von Gerkan
Partner Nikolaus Goetze
Design team Dirk Heller,
Karen Schroeder, Meike
Schmidt, Friedhelm Chlosta,
Christoph Berle, Wencke
Eissing, Georg Traun,
Kai Siebke, Holger Wermers
Client Beijing Yin Xin Guang
Hua Real Estate Development
PTY Ltd.
Gross floor area
800,000 m²

Chaofu Avenue, Beijing
Consultancy 2002
Design Meinhard von Gerkan
Design team Hinrich Müller,
Gregor Hoheisel, Udo Meyer,
David Schenke, Gero
Heimann, Jing Jun Zhou,
Yun Fang Xu
Client Beijing Municipal
Planning Commission
Gross floor area
1,876,000 m²

Opera House, Guangzhou
Competition 2002
Design Meinhard von Gerkan
with Klaus Lenz
Design team Dominik Reh,
Jörn Herrmann, Svenia
Oehmig, Hauke Petersen,
Kai Ladebeck, Hung-Wei Hsu,
Sandra Glass
Client The Organizing
Committee of Architectural
Design Competition by
International Invitation for
Guangzhou Opera House
Gross floor area 73,000 m²

**Siemens China
Headquarters, Beijing**
Consultancy 2002,
2nd prize
Design Meinhard von Gerkan
Design team Doris Schäffler,
Giuseppina Orto, Nicolas
Pomränke, David Schenke
Client Siemens Real Estate
Gross floor area 110,000 m²

Wanda Plaza, Beijing
Hotel and office complex
Competition 2002, 1st prize
Design Volkwin Marg and
Hubert Nienhoff
Project managers Alexander
Buchhofer, Silvia Schneider
Design team Christian
Dorndorf, Martin Duplantier,
Xia Lin, Nicolas Pomränke
Project team (Façade
design) Veit Lieneweg, Stefan
Rewolle, Du Peng, Chunsong
Dong
Chinese partner practice
Jianghe Group
Gross floor area
130,000 m²
Construction period
2005–2007

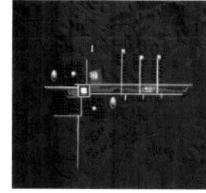

**Renmin University of
Zhuhai**
Competition 2002
Design Meinhard von Gerkan
Partner Nikolaus Goetze
Design team Volkmar
Sievers, Simone Nentwig, Jörn
Bohlmann, Huan Zhu, Nicole
Loeffler, Rouven Oberdiek, Leif
Henning
Client Renmin University
Gross floor area
1,137,000 m²

Shunchi Plaza, Tianjin
Urban planning
Competition 2002
Design Meinhard von Gerkan
with Stephan Schütz, Stephan
Rewolle and Kristian
Uthe-Spencker
Partner Hubert Nienhoff
Design team Michèle Rüegg,
Patrick Pfleiderer, Uta Graff,
Christian Dorndorf, Markus
Pfisterer, Helga Reimund,
Martin Duplantier
Client Tianjin Shunchi
Investment Co., Ltd.
Gross floor area
110,000 m²

Beijing Château, Beijing
Luxury apartment building
Design Meinhard von Gerkan
with Magdalene Weiß, 2002
Partner Nikolaus Goetze
Design and project team
Michèle Watenphul, Kai
Ladebeck, Holger Schmücker,
Xia Lin, Gregor Hoheisel,
Stephanie Heß, Iris van Hülst,
Sigrid Müller, Jörn Ortmann,
Marcus Tanzen, Hito Ueda,
Holger Wermers
Chinese partner practice
Central Research Institute of
Building and Construction
Design of M.M.I
Client Beijing Shoulu-
Huayuan Property Co., Ltd.
Gross floor area 69,000 m²
Construction period
2003–2008

Lingang New City
Competition 2002, 1st prize
Design Meinhard von Gerkan
Partner Nikolaus Goetze
Design team Jessica Weber,
Annika Schröder, Beate
Quaschning, Christoph
Böttinger, Wei Wu, Sigrid
Müller, Eduard Kaiser,
Hung-Wei Hsu, Richard
Sprenger, Stephanie Heß,
Christian Krüger, Hector Labin,
Markus Carlsen
Port planning HPC Hamburg
Port Consulting
Landscape architects
Breimann & Bruun
Light planning Schlotfeldt
Licht

Client Shanghai Harbour City
Development (Group) Co., Ltd.
Mr. Bao Tieming
Area 74,000 m²
Inhabitants 800,000
Construction period
2003–2020

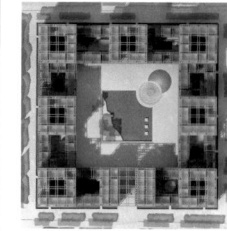

**University of Aeronautics
and Astronautics, Beijing**
Competition 2003, 1st prize
Design Meinhard von Gerkan
Partner Joachim Zais
Design team Tanja Gutena,
Sigrid Müller, Julia Künzer, Kai
Ladebeck, Dominik Reh,
Matias Otto, Mike Berrier, Jörn
Herrmann, Hauke Petersen
Client Beijing University of
Aeronautics and Astronautics
Gross floor area
620,000 m²

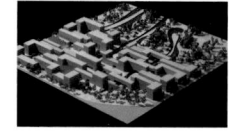

**Electron Administrative
Affair Center, Beijing**
Competition 2003
Design Meinhard von Gerkan
with Nicolas Hünerwadel
Partner Nikolaus Goetze
Design team Sigrid Müller,
Annika Schröder, Markus
Carlsen, Jörn Herrmann,
Hung-Wei Hsu, Sona Kazemi,
Stephanie Heß, Richard
Sprenger
Client Beijing Wanjing Real
Estate Development Co., Ltd.
Gross floor area
175,000 m²

**Science Park of the
University of Zhejiang**
Urban planning
Competition 2003, 1st prize
Design Meinhard von Gerkan
with Walter Gebhardt
Project manager
Volkmar Sievers
Design and project team
Simone Nentwig, Christian
Krüger, Arne Kleinhans,
Rouven Oberdiek, Evelyn
Pasdzierny, Matthias Ismael,
Niko Rickert, Hinrich Müller,
Hauke Petersen
Chinese partner practice
ZUADR, Architectural Design
and Research Institute of
Zhejiang University
Client Zhejiang University
Science Park Construction Co.,
Ltd.
Gross floor area
297,000 m²

**Gongyuan Building in
Hangzhou**
Design Meinhard von Gerkan,
2003
Partner Nikolaus Goetze
Project manager Volkmar
Sievers
Design and project team
Simone Nentwig, Huan Zhu,
Andrea Moritz, Knut Maass,
Rouven Oberdiek,

Tobias Plinke, Nicole Loeffler, Wiebke Dorn, Nils Dethlefs, Kerstin Steinfatt, Jörn Bohlmann
Client Hangzhou Nice Source United Real Estate Co., Ltd.
Chinese partner practice ZADRI
Gross floor area 123,000 m²
Construction period 2003–2006

Husian Live Science and Technology Park, Wuxi
Competition 2003
Design Meinhard von Gerkan with Magdalene Weiß
Design team Michèle Watenphul, Kai Ladebeck, Jun Wen, Holger Schmücker, Evagelia Segkis
Client Wuxi Live SCI & Tech. Development Co., Ltd.
Gross floor area 10,000 m²

Shenzhen Central Plaza
Urban planning
Competition 2003, one 1st prize
Design Meinhard von Gerkan with Doris Schäffler and Stephan Schütz
Design team Giuseppina Orto, David Schenke
Client Shenzhen Guanghai Investment Co., Ltd.
Gross floor area 161,500 m²

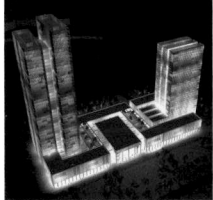

Dong Cheng International Center, Nanjing
Competition 2003, 1st prize
Design Meinhard von Gerkan
Design team Volkmar Sievers, Simone Nentwig, Huan Zhu, Nicole Loeffler, Tobias Plinke, Leif Henning, Christian Krüger, Wei Wu
Client Jiangsu Rendi Property Development Company Ltd. Yurun Group
Gross floor area 188,000 m²

Qinghe Jade Residences, Beijing
Survey 2003
Design Meinhard von Gerkan
Partner Nikolaus Goetze
Design team Stephanie Heß, Hinrich Müller, Mike Berrier, Hung-Wei Hsu, Richard Sprenger
Client Beijing Qiangyou Real Estate Development Co.
Gross floor area 1,000,000 m²

Nanxiang Central Town
Urban Planning
Competition 2003
Design Meinhard von Gerkan
Partner Joachim Zais

Design team Sigrid Müller, Jörn Herrmann, Hector Labin, Monika van Vught
Gross floor area 3,000,000 m²

Dixingju Office Building, Beijing
Consultancy 2003
Design Meinhard von Gerkan with Doris Schäffler and Stephan Schütz
Design and project team David Schenke, Chunsong Dong
Chinese partner practice CABR, Building Design Institute – China Academy of Building Research
Client Beijing Shoulu-Huayuan Property Co., Ltd.
Gross floor area 33,000 m²
Construction period 2004–2006

Convention & Exhibition Center, Suzhou
Competition 2003, 3rd prize
Design Volkwin Marg with Marc Ziemons
Partner Nikolaus Goetze
Design team Dirk Balser, Christiane Fickers, Hung-Wei Hsu, Udo Meyer
Client Suzhou Industrial Park Housing & Development Co., Ltd.
Gross floor area 300,000 m²

Qingdao Sailing Base for the Olympic Games 2008
Competition 2003
Design Meinhard von Gerkan with Walter Gebhardt
Design team Matthias Ismael, Enno Maass, Hinrich Müller, Evelyn Pasdzierny, Christoph Thomsen
Client Qingdao Development & Construction Group Corporation
Gross floor area 730,000 m²

Orient Wenhua Art Center, Beijing
Hyatt Regency Hotel, culture hall and office complex
Competition 2003
Design Meinhard von Gerkan and Stephan Schütz
Project management David Schenke, Lin Lin Jiang
Design and project team Ralf Sieber, Na Zhang, Ran Li, Daniela Franz
Client Beijing Oriental Continent Real Estate Development and Management Co., Ltd.
Gross floor area 140,000 m²
Construction period 2006–2008

National Stadium for the Olympic Games 2008, Beijing
Competition 2003
Design Volkwin Marg with Hubert Nienhoff and Markus Pfisterer
Design team Christian Dorndorf, Uta Graff, Jochen Köhn, Katina Roloff, Anke Rieber, Silvia Schneider, Caspar Teichgräber, Helga Reimund, Holger Betz
Client Beijing Municipal Government

Lanhai Hotel, Jinan
Competition 2003, 1st prize
Design Meinhard von Gerkan with Stephan Schütz and Doris Schäffler
Design and project team Chunsong Dong, Gero Heimann, Giuseppina Orto, Nicolas Pomränke, David Schenke
Client Shan Dong Lanhai Stock Co., Ltd.
Gross floor area 57,000 m²

Jinglun Hotel, Beijing
Façade study 2003
Design Meinhard von Gerkan
Design team Stephan Schütz, Nicolas Pomränke

Science Center Guangdong, Guangzhou
Competition 2003
Design Meinhard von Gerkan
Partner Nikolaus Goetze
Design team Evelyn Pasdzierny, Tobias Jortzick, Arne Kleinhans, Jörn Herrmann, Christian Krüger, Rouven Oberdiek
Client Guangdong Provincial Department of Science & Technology
Gross floor area 115,000 m²

Nansha Business Center, Guangzhou
Competition 2003
Design Meinhard von Gerkan
Design team Evelyn Pasdzierny, Matthias Ismael, Niko Rickert, Hinrich Müller, Matthias Meinheit, Elena Melnykova, Alexander Behn, Henry Rodatz
Client Guangzhou Nansha Assets Operation Co., Ltd.
Gross floor area 300,000 m²

Shooting Range for the Olympic Games 2008, Beijing
Competition 2003
Design Volkwin Marg with Marc Ziemons
Partner Nikolaus Goetze
Design team Dirk Balser, Christiane Fickers, Hung-Wei Hsu, David Schenke, Meike Schmidt, Flori Wagner
Client State General Administration of Sports of P.R. China
Gross floor area 40,000 m²

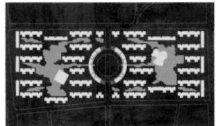

Olympic Village & National Gymnasium, Beijing
Competition 2003
Design Meinhard von Gerkan and Nikolaus Goetze with Walter Gebhardt
Design team Hinrich Müller, Enno Maass
Client Beijing Beichen Real Estate Co., Ltd.

Zhongguancun International City, Beijing
Office and commercial building with hotel
Competition 2003
Design Meinhard von Gerkan
Design team Doris Schäffler, Stephan Schütz, Giuseppina Orto, Nicolas Pomränke
Client Gulf Group Gulf Land Development Co., Ltd.
Gross floor area 79,500 m²

Human Resource Center, Shenzhen
Consultancy 2003
Design Meinhard von Gerkan with Walter Gebhardt
Partner Nikolaus Goetze
Design team Jan Stecher, Matthias Meinheit
Client SZRC
Gross floor area 43,000m²

China Telecom Information Park, Shanghai
Master plan
Competition 2003, 1st prize
Design Meinhard von Gerkan
Partner Nikolaus Goetze
Design team Evelyn Pasdzierny, Matthias Meinheit, Tilo Günther, Eduard Kaiser
Client China Telecom Group Co., Ltd.
Gross floor area 550,000 m²
Construction period 2005–2012

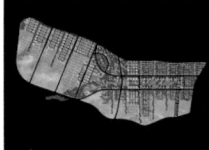

Dalian Airport City, Dalian
Competition 2003, 1st prize
Design Meinhard von Gerkan with Walter Gebhardt
Design team Alexander Behn, Niko Rickert, Henry Rodatz, Jan Stecher

Client Urban Planning Bureau of Gangjingzi District, City of Dalian
Gross floor area 7,683,000 m²

National Library of China, Beijing
Competition 2003
Design Meinhard von Gerkan
Partner Nikolaus Goetze
Design team Karen Schroeder, Dirk Heller, Christoph Berle, Georg Traun, Friedhelm Chlosta, Meike Schmidt, Kai Siebke, Wencke Eissing, Rouven Oberdiek
Client Preparatory Office for National Library of China
Gross floor area 77,000 m²

CYTS Tower, Beijing
Office building of China Youth Travel Service
Design Meinhard von Gerkan with Stephan Schütz and Doris Schäffler, 2003
Design and project team Nicolas Pomränke, Giuseppina Orto, Lan Chen, Anette Löber, Ralf Sieber
Structural engineers Schlaich, Bergermann and Partners
Chinese partner practice CABR
Client China CYTS Tours Holding Co., Ltd.
Gross floor area 65,000 m²
Construction period 2004–2006

Agricultural Bank of China, Shanghai
Computing center
Competition 2003
Design Meinhard von Gerkan with Walter Gebhardt
Partners Joachim Zais, Jürgen Hillmer
Design team Jan Stecher, Richard Sprenger, Markus Carlsen, Alexander Behn
Client Agricultural Bank of China (ABC)
Gross floor area 90,000 m²

Yanlord Plaza, Chengdu
Office and commercial Building
Design Meinhard von Gerkan, 2003
Partner Nikolaus Goetze
Design team Karen Schroeder, Dirk Heller, Christoph Berle, Wencke Eissing, Kai Siebke, Friedhelm Chlosta, Meike Schmidt, Markus Carlsen, Udo Meyer, Georg Traun
Client Yanlord Industrial (Chengdu) Co. Ltd.
Gross floor area 250,000 m²

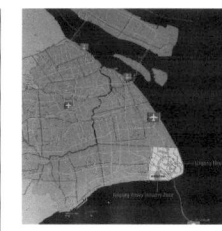

Lingang Development District
Urban extension of Lingang New City
Competition 2003
Design Meinhard von Gerkan
Partner Joachim Zais
Design team Sigrid Müller, Annika Schröder, Heiko Thiess, Julia Künzer, Matthias Ismael, Jan Blasko, Hinrich Müller, Markus Carlsen, Hung-Wei Hsu, Richard Sprenger, Dominik Reh, Tanja Gutena
Client Shanghai Lingang Economic Development (Group) Co., Ltd.
Area 293,000 m²

Beijing New Vision International Exhibition Center
Competition 2003, 2nd prize
Design Volkwin Marg with Marc Ziemons
Partner Nikolaus Goetze
Design team Udo Meyer, Hung-Wei Hsu, Dirk Balser, Alexander Behn
Client Beijing New Vision International Exhibition Center Co., Ltd.
Gross floor area 150,000 m²

Foshan Central Area
Urban planning
Competition 2003
Design Meinhard von Gerkan
Design team Enno Maass, Peter Glaser, Thomas Krautwald, Martin Tamke, Norbert Freitag, Jan Schiemann, Björn Seegebarth, Enno Mohr
Client Beijing Beichen Real Estate Co., Ltd.

Century Lotus Sports Park with Stadium and Swimming Hall, Foshan
Competition 2003, 2nd prize
Design Volkwin Marg with Christian Hoffmann
Partner Nikolaus Goetze
Project manager Christian Hoffmann
Design team Marek Nowak, Christoph Helbich, Mario Rojas Toledo, Michael König, Sven Greiser, Sebastian Hilke, Mark Jackschat
Project team Michael Haase, Stephan Menke, Franz Lensing, Björn Füchtenkord, Sven Greiser, Silke Flaßnöcker, Ebi Tang, Jennifer Kielas
Structural engineers Schlaich, Bergermann and Partners
Client Foshan Sports Site Construction Center for the 12th Provincial Sports Event

Chinese partner practice
South China University,
Architectural Design and
Research Institute
Seats stadium 36,000
Seats swimming hall 2,800
Construction period
2004–2006

Software Park, Dalian
Competition 2003
Design Meinhard von Gerkan
with Walter Gebhardt
Design team Elena
Melnikova, Jan Stecher, Tobias
Jortzick, Christian Dahle, Julia
Gronbach, Janis Guida
Client China International
Engineering Consulting
Corporation
Gross floor area
4,000,000 m²

**Gold Tak Center,
Guangzhou**
Competition 2003
Design Meinhard von Gerkan
Design team Enno Maass,
Richard Sprenger, Hung-Wei
Hsu, Julia Künzer, Markus
Carlsen, Thomas Esper,
Caroline Kolb, Jan Blasko
Client Gold Sun Group,
Guangzhou

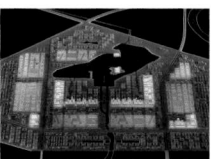

New Central Area, Xuzhou
Urban planning
Competition 2003
Design Meinhard von Gerkan
Design team Enno Maass,
Richard Sprenger, Hung-Wei
Hsu, Matthias Meinheit
Client City of Xuzhou
Gross floor area 83,300 m²

**International Medical
Garden, Shanghai**
Competition 2003
Design Meinhard von Gerkan
and Joachim Zais
Design team Heiko Thiess,
Richard Sprenger, Robert
Friedrichs, Monika van Vught,
Matthias Ismael, Matias Otto,
Xuelai Xu
Client International Medicine
Garden Co. Ltd.
Gross floor area 1.15 ha

Grand Theater, Chongqing
Competition 2003, 1st prize
Design Meinhard von Gerkan
Partner Nikolaus Goetze
Project manager Volkmar
Sievers
Design team Heiko Thiess,
Monika van Vught, Robert
Friedrichs, Matthias Ismael,
Tobias Jortzick, Dominik Reh,
Christian Dahle, Julia
Gronbach
Project team Knut Maass,
Huan Zhu, Kerstin Steinfatt,
Jan Stolte, Nils Dethlefs
Chinese partner practice
ECADI

Client Chongqing Urban
Construction Investment
Gross floor area 100,000 m²
Construction period
2005–2009

Phoenix TV, Shenzhen
Design Volkwin Marg, 2003
Partner Nikolaus Goetze
Design team Marc Ziemons,
Christiane Fickers, Flori
Wagner, Dirk Balser,
Hung-Wei Hsu, Janis Guida
Client Phoenix Satellite TV
Ltd., Hongkong
Gross floor area
107,300 m²

**Twin Towers and CBD
Xinghai Bay, Dalian**
Competition 2003, 1st prize
Design Meinhard von Gerkan
Partner Nikolaus Goetze
Project managers Karen
Schroeder, Dirk Heller
Design and project team
Christoph Berle, Friedhelm
Chlosta, Kai Siebke, Holger
Schmücker, Sabrina Wilms,
Katharina Traupe, Georg Traun,
Meike Schmidt, Markus
Carlsen, Eduard Kaiser,
Christian Dahle, Udo Meyer,
Wencke Eissing-Poggenberg
Chinese partner practice
ECADI
Client Dalian Commodity
Exchange
Gross floor area
353,000 m²
**Construction period of
Tower A** 2004–2008
**Construction period of
Tower B** until 2009
**Construction period of
adjoining building (5-star
Howard Johnson hotel with
300 rooms)** until 2007

**China Petroleum
Headquarters, Beijing**
Competition 2003
Design Meinhard von Gerkan
with Stephan Schütz
Design team Nicolas
Pomränke, Giuseppina Orto,
Gero Heimann, Chunsong
Dong

**Xi Han Grand Building,
Beijing**
Competition 2003
Design Meinhard von Gerkan
with Stephan Schütz and Doris
Schäffler
Design team Yi Wang,
Yingzhe Wang, Ralf Sieber
Gross floor area
100,000 m²

Art Box, Beijing
Competition 2003
Design Meinhard von Gerkan
with Stephan Schütz
Design team David Schenke,
Katrin Kanus
Client Stiftung für Kunst
und Kultur, Bonn/Germany
Gross floor area 58,900 m²

**De Sheng Men Center,
Beijing**
Office complex
Study 2003
Design Meinhard von Gerkan
and Stephan Schütz with
Christian Dorndorf
Gross floor area
240,000 m²

**International Sailing Marina
for the 29th Olympic
Games, Qingdao**
Competition 2004
Design Meinhard von Gerkan
with Walter Gebhard
Design team Holger
Henningsen, Christian
Scheelk, Gordon Schittek,
Britta Schröder, Felix Wiesner
Client Qingdao Urban
Planning Bureau
Gross floor area 77,000 m²

Huaneng Building, Beijing
Competition 2004,
one 1st prize
Design Meinhard von Gerkan
with Stephan Schütz
Design team Stephan
Rewolle, Chunsong Dong,
Katrin Kanus, Ralf Sieber,
Du Peng
Client China Huaneng Group
Gross floor area
130,000 m²

**New Maritime University,
Shanghai**
Competition 2004,
one 1st prize
Design Meinhard von Gerkan
Design team Heiko Thiess,
Claudia Schultze, Markus
Carlsen, Eduard Kaiser
Client New Maritime
University, Shanghai
Gross floor area
1,333,000 m²

**"Cloud Needle",
Lingang New City**
Study 2004
Design Meinhard von Gerkan
with Richard Sprenger
Design team Heiko Thiess,
Enno Maass, Eduard Kaiser
Client Shanghai Urban
Planning Administration
Bureau, Mr. Bao Tieming
Height 300 m

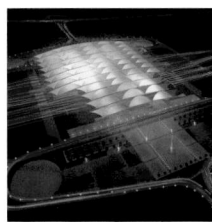

New Railway Station, Guangzhou
Competition 2004, 2nd prize
Design Meinhard von Gerkan
Partner Jürgen Hillmer
Design team Volkmar Sievers, Sigrid Müller, Christian Dahle, Tilo Günther, Matthias Meinheit, Simone Nentwig, Rouven Oberdiek, Nicole Loeffler, Susi Winter, Huan Zhu
Client Guangzhou Railway (Group) Corporation
Gross floor area 342,000 m²

New China International Exhibition Center, Beijing
Competition 2004
Design Volkwin Marg
Partner Nikolaus Goetze
Design team Christiane Fickers, Flori Wagner, Dirk Balser, Hinrich Müller, Matthias Ismael
Client China International Exhibition Center Investment & Development Co., Ltd.
Gross floor area 340,000 m²

Hotel Oriental Art Center, Shanghai
Competition 2004
Design Meinhard von Gerkan
Partner Nikolaus Goetze
Design team Volkmar Sievers, Huan Zhu, Matthias Meinheit, Simone Nentwig, Nicole Loeffler, Andrea Moritz
Client Shanghai Pudong Land Development (Holding) Corp.
Gross floor area 27,000 m²

National Tennis Center and Hockey Stadium, Beijing
Design Volkwin Marg, 2004
Partner Nikolaus Goetze
Design team Marc Ziemons, Dirk Balser, Christiane Fickers, Flori Wagner, Katja Zoschke, Carsten Plog, Janis Guida
Organizer Beijing Municipal Planning Commission
Gross floor area 67,200 m²

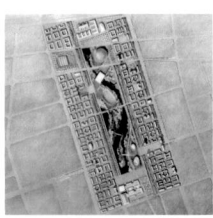

Loudun-Shahe, Education Center, Beijing
Study 2004
Design Meinhard von Gerkan
Partner Stephan Schütz
Design team Sophie Baumann, Kristian Uthe-Spencker

Sheshan Erzhan Station of Shanghai No 9, Shanghai
Competition 2004
Design Meinhard von Gerkan
Partner Nikolaus Goetze

Design team Magdalene Weiß, Christian Dahle, Enno Maass, Elena Melnikova, Hinrich Müller, Jan Stecher, Stephanie Heß
Client CITIC
Gross floor area 90,000 m²

Science Park, Ningbo
Competition 2004
Design Meinhard von Gerkan
Partner Nikolaus Goetze
Design team Volkmar Sievers, Simone Nentwig, Rouven Oberdiek, Nicole Loeffler, Kay-Peter Kolbe, Uli Rösler
Client GREENTOWN, Hangzhou
Gross floor area 140,000 m²

Riverfront Cultural Park, Changsha
Competition 2004
Design Meinhard von Gerkan
Design team Hinrich Müller, Evelyn Pasdzierny, Elena Melnikova, Eduard Kaiser, Rouven Oberdiek, Tilo Günther, Markus Carlsen
Gross floor area 175,000 m²

National Museum of China, Beijing
Competition 2004, 1st prize
Design Meinhard von Gerkan with Stephan Schütz, Stephan Rewolle and Doris Schäffler
Design team Gregor Hoheisel, Katrin Kanus, Ralf Sieber, Du Peng, Chunsong Dong
Project team Matthias Wiegelmann, Patrick Pfleiderer, Helga Reimund, Tobias Keyl, Anna Bulanda, Christian Dorndorf, Ulli Bachmann, Ajda Guelbahar, Johanna Enzinger, Verena Fischbach, Wei Bao, Yang Liu, Lin Xia
Chinese partner practice CABR
Client National Museum of China
Gross floor area 170,000 m²
Construction period 2007–2010

Zhongguancun Christian Church, Haidian District, Beijing
Competition 2004, 1st prize
Design Meinhard von Gerkan
Partner Stephan Schütz
Design and project team Stephan Rewolle, Lin Xia, Helga Reimund, Gero Heimann, Katrin Kanus, Ralf Sieber, Gregor Hoheisel
Chinese partner practice Sunlight Architects and Engineers Co., Ltd.

Client China Zhongguancun Culture Development Co., Ltd.
Gross floor area 4,000 m²
Construction period 2005–2007

Marriott Hotel, Binjiang Plaza, Ningbo
Competition 2004, 1st prize
Design Meinhard von Gerkan
Partner Nikolaus Goetze
Project manager Volkmar Sievers
Design and project team Simone Nentwig, Matthias Meinheit, Martina Klostermann, Rouven Oberdiek, Knut Maass, Nicole Loeffler, Uli Rösler, Evelyn Pasdzierny, Nils Dethlefs, Tilo Günther
Chinese partner practice CJY
Client Ningbo HaiCheng Investment Development Co., Ltd.
Gross floor area 89,600 m²
Construction period 2005–2008

Automobile Electronic Industry Park, Beijing
Competition 2004, 1st prize
Design Meinhard von Gerkan
Partner Stephan Schütz
Design team Giuseppina Orto, Nicolas Pomränke, Christian Dorndorf, Bin Bin Du, Sophie Baumann
Client Majuqiao Town Government of Tongzhou District, Beijing
Gross floor area 2,896,000 m²

New Railway Station, Wuhan
Competition 2004, 4th place
Design Meinhard von Gerkan
Partner Jürgen Hillmer
Design team Sigrid Müller, Christiane Fickers, Dirk Balser, Diana Spanier, Janis Guida
Client Zhengzhou Railway Administration
Gross floor area 94,000 m²

West Railway Station, Tianjin
Competition 2004, 1st prize
Design Meinhard von Gerkan and Stephan Schütz with Nicolas Pomränke
Design team Ralf Sieber, Xu Ji, Jochen Sültrup, Christian Dorndorf, Bernd Gotthardt, Sabine Stage, Cai Wei
Client TSDI Tianjin Ministry of Railway
Gross floor area 52,386 m² (aboveground)

Management and Service Center of Lingang New City Hotel, bank and office complex
Competition 2004, 1st prize
Design Meinhard von Gerkan with Magdalene Weiß
Partners Nikolaus Goetze, Wei Wu
Design and project team Jan Stecher, Jörn Ortmann, Xiangge Peng, Yang Li, Mo Song, Enno Maass, Wang Yingzhe, Wang Yi
Chinese partner practice SIMEE
Client Shanghai Lingang Economic Development Group Co., Ltd.
Gross floor area 45,000 m²
Construction period 2004–2005

Guangzhou Twin Towers
Competition 2004
Design Meinhard von Gerkan
Partner Nikolaus Goetze
Design team Volkmar Sievers, Evelyn Pasdzierny, Rouven Oberdiek, Alexandra Kühne, Matthias Meinheit, Nicole Loeffler
Client Guangzhou Municipal Land Development Center
Gross floor area 372,000 m²

Ningbo New Town
Design Meinhard von Gerkan, 2004
Partners Nikolaus Goetze, Wei Wu
Design team Magdalene Weiß, Jan Stecher, Yi Wang
Client Ningbo Planning Bureau
Gross floor area 620,000 m²

NBCT Exhibition Center District, Ningbo
Competition 2004
Design Meinhard von Gerkan
Partner Wei Wu
Design team Magdalene Weiß, Hung-Wei Hsu, Yi Wang, Yingzhe Wang
Client NBCT
Gross floor area 400,000 m²

East China Power Central Building, Shanghai
Competition 2004
Design Meinhard von Gerkan
Partner Nikolaus Goetze
Design team Karen Schroeder, Dirk Heller, Christoph Berle, Meike Schmidt, Friedhelm Chlosta, Kai Siebke, Georg Traun, Hung-Wei Hsu, Matthias Meinheit, Holger Schmücker, Matthias Ismael, Nina Lhotzki, Xuelai Xu

Client East China Power Dispatch Central Building
Gross floor area 50,000 m²

Grand Theater, Qingdao Opera house with hotel, media and conference center
Competition 2004, 1st prize
Design Meinhard von Gerkan and Stephan Schütz with Nicolas Pomränke
Design and project team Clemens Kampermann, Johannes Erdmann, Kian Lian, Gerd Meyer, Chongsong Dong, Li Ling, Annette Löber, Xin Meng, Jochen Sültrup, Sophie von Mansberg
Chinese partner practice ECADI
Client Qingdao Conson Industrial Corporation
Gross floor area 80,000 m²
Opera hall 1,600 seats
Concert hall 1,200 seats
Multifunctional hall 400 seats
Construction period 2005–2008

Shi Liu Pu, Shanghai Urban planning
Competition 2004, 1st prize
Design Meinhard von Gerkan with Stephan Schütz
Design team Stephan Rewolle, Du Peng, Katrin Kanus, Ralf Sieber
Client Huangpu River Group

Lingang New City, New Bund
Consultancy 2004
Design Meinhard von Gerkan
Partner Nikolaus Goetze
Design team Annika Schröder, Barbara Henke, Diana Spanier, Christian Dahle, Eduard Kaiser, Markus Carlsen, Ben Grope
Client Shanghai Harbour City Development (Group) Co., Ltd.
Gross floor area 320,000 m²

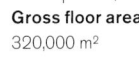

Lingang New City, Western Island
Consultancy 2004
Design Meinhard von Gerkan
Partner Nikolaus Goetze
Design team Evelyn Pasdzierny, Alexandra Kühne, Markus Carlsen
Client Shanghai Harbour City Development (Group) Co., Ltd.
Gross floor area 135,000 m²

Jinling Library, Nanjing
Competition 2004
Design Meinhard von Gerkan
Partner Nikolaus Goetze
Design team Evelyn Pasdzierny, Alexandra Kühne, Barbara Henke, Yinzhe Wang, Yi Wang, Jörn Ortmann
Client Nanjing National Assets Cultural Industry Co., Ltd.
Gross floor area 25,000 m²

Ministry of Commerce, Beijing
Competition 2004, 2nd prize
Design Meinhard von Gerkan
Partner Stephan Schütz
Design team Stephan Rewolle, Du Peng, Kathrin Kanus, Ralf Sieber, Iris Belle, Dongchun Song, David Schenke

China Telecom, Building 1, Shanghai
Competition 2004
Design Meinhard von Gerkan
Partner Nikolaus Goetze
Design team Dirk Heller, Karen Schroeder, Meike Schmidt, Kai Siebke, Friedhelm Chlosta, Christoph Berle, Georg Traun, Holger Schmücker, Nina Lhotzky, Hung-Wei Hsu
Client China Telecom Shanghai
Gross floor area 37,200 m²

CSSC Shanghai Shipyard, Pudong
Competition 2004
Design Meinhard von Gerkan
Partners Nikolaus Goetze, Wei Wu
Design team Magdalene Weiß, Yinzhe Wang, Yi Wang, Hung-Wei Hsu, Annika Schröder, Li Yang

Convention and Exhibition Center, Xiamen
Competition 2004
Design Volkwin Marg
Partner Nikolaus Goetze
Design team Hinrich Müller, Heiko Thiess, Richard Sprenger, Diana Spanier, Elena Melnikova, Ben Grope, Markus Carlsen
Client Jianfa Group Real Estate
Gross floor area 54,500 m²

Guotai Theater, Chongqing
Competition 2005
Design Meinhard von Gerkan
with Volkmar Sievers
Partner Nikolaus Goetze
Design team Andrea Moritz,
Sabrina Fienemann, Tilo
Günther, Rouven Oberdiek
Client Chongqing Real Estate
Group
Gross floor area 44,000 m²

**Hui Jia Education Center,
Beijing**
**Office building with book
store and conference area**
Design Meinhard von Gerkan
and Stephan Schütz , 2005
Project management David
Schenke
Design and project team
Lin Lin Jiang, Na Zhang
Chinese partner practice
BIAD, Beijing
Client Hui Jia Education
Group
Gross floor area 21,500 m²
Construction period
2007–2009

**Shanghai Yuexing Global
Home Furnishing Expo
Center**
Competition 2005
Design Meinhard von Gerkan
Design team Magdalene
Weiß, Enno Maass, Mo Song,
Yi Lin
Client Yuexing Group
Gross floor area
36,000,000 m²

**Research and Development
Center, Beijing**
Consultancy 2005
Design Meinhard von Gerkan
Partner Stephan Schütz
Design team Giuseppina
Orto, Patrick Pfleiderer,
Tobias Keyl, Nicolas Pomränke,
Ji Xu
Gross floor area
137,900 m²

**Shanghai Industrial Health
Park**
Competition 2005, 1st prize
Design Meinhard von Gerkan
with Walter Gebhardt
Partner Nikolaus Goetze
Design team Holger
Henningsen, Gordon Schittek,
Nicole Döhr, Michael Sue,
Simon Braun,
Monika Sorokowska
Client Tianshi Yihai Co., Ltd.
Gross floor area
600,000 m²

**Headquarters of the China
Development Bank, Beijing**
Competition 2005
Design Meinhard von Gerkan
and Stephan Schütz

Design team Giuseppina
Orto, Clemens Kampermann,
Tobias Keyl, Meng Xin, Ji Xu
Client China Development
Bank
Gross floor area 150,000 m²

**Shanghai Nanhui District
Administrative Office
Center, Lingang New City**
Competition 2005, 1st prize
Design Meinhard von Gerkan
Partner Nikolaus Goetze
Project management
Jörn Ortmann
Design team Li Yang,
Mo Song, Xiange Peng, Yanli
Hao, Chen Fu, Evelyn
Pasdzierny, Alexandra Kühne,
Barbara Henke
Chinese partner practice
SIADR
Client Government of the
Nanhui District
Gross floor area
100,860 m²
Construction period
2006–2008

**Business Center, Hou Ren
Road, Hangzhou**
Competition 2005
Design Meinhard von Gerkan
Partner Nikolaus Goetze
Design team Volkmar
Sievers, Simone Nentwig,
Jan Stolte, Wiebke Meyenburg
Client Hangzhou Canhigh
Estate Co.
Gross floor area
130,000 m²

**International Convention
and Exhibition Center,
Shenyang**
Competition 2005
Design Volkwin Marg
Partner Nikolaus Goetze
Design team Marc Ziemons,
Hinrich Müller, Flori Wagner,
Katrin Löser, Henning Fritsch,
Kristina Milani
Client Shenyang Zhi Cheng
Tendering Co., Ltd
Gross floor area
456,000 m²

**Office Building, Wanxiang
Plaza, Shanghai-Pudong**
Competition 2005, 1st prize
Design Meinhard von Gerkan
Partner Nikolaus Goetze
Project manager
Volkmar Sievers
Design team Evelyn
Pasdzierny, Alexandra Kühne,
Barbara Henke
Project team Diana Spanier,
Andrea Moritz, Christian
Krüger
Chinese partner practice
HSA Huasen Hangzhou
Client Wanxiang Group
Corporation
Gross floor area 35,000 m²
Construction period
2007–2009

**Hualian Twin Towers,
Hangzhou**
Design Meinhard von Gerkan,
2005
Partner Nikolaus Goetze
Project management
Volkmar Sievers
Design and project team
Simone Nentwig, Wiebke
Meyenburg, Diana Spanier,
Uli Rösler, Alexandra Kühne,
Barbara Henke
Chinese partner practice
Zhejiang Chenjian
Development, Hangzhou
Client UNION DEVELOPING
GROUP OF CHINA,
Hangzhou
Gross floor area
122,800 m²
Height 137 m
Construction period
2006–2008

**Shimao Twin Towers,
Shanghai-Pudong**
Competition 2005
Design Meinhard von Gerkan
Partner Nikolaus Goetze
Design team Hinrich Müller,
Katrin Loeser, Christian
Schwister, Michèle Watenphul,
Matthias Mumm, Markus
Carlsen, Jürgen Krieger,
Elena Melnikowa
Client Shimao Group
Gross floor area
388,000 m²

**Hainan Sanya National
Hotel**
Competition 2005, 3rd prize
Design Meinhard von Gerkan
Partner Wei Wu
Design team Magdalene
Weiß, Annika Schröder,
Hung-Wei Shu, Yi Wang,
Yinzhe Wang
Client Hainan State Estate
Gross floor area 72,000 m²

Jinsha Museum, Chengdu
Competition 2005
Design Meinhard von Gerkan
with Stephan Schütz and
Stephan Rewolle
Design team Ralf Sieber Iris
Belle, Bin Zhou, Lei Wang,
Katrin Kanus, David Schenke
Gross floor area 28,500 m²

**Wuqing Health Industrial
Park, Tianjin**
Consultancy 2005
Design Meinhard von Gerkan
Partner Nikolaus Goetze
Design team Evelyn
Pasdzierny, Richard Sprenger,
Alexandra Kühne
Client Tiens Group Co., Ltd.
Gross floor area 200,000 m²

City Gates, Lingang New City
Design Meinhard von Gerkan with Richard Sprenger, 2005
Partner Nikolaus Goetze
Client Shanghai Harbour City Investment Co.

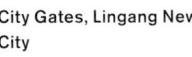

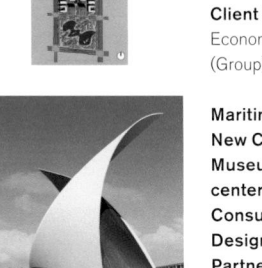

Heavy Industry Zone, Lingang
Consultancy 2005
Design Meinhard von Gerkan with Magdalene Weiß
Partner Wei Wu
Design team Hung-Wei Hsu
Client Shanghai Lingang Economic Development (Group) Co., Ltd.

Maritime Museum, Lingang New City
Museum, library and youth center
Consultancy 2005
Design Meinhard von Gerkan
Partner Nikolaus Goetze
Project managers Klaus Lenz, Marcus Tanzen
Design and project team Richard Sprenger, Eazy Lin, Jens Reichert, Birgit Föllmer, Udo Meyer, Elena Melnikova, Ben Grope, Markus Carlsen
Chinese partner practice SIADR
Client Shanghai Harbour City Investment Co.
Gross floor area 72,400 m²
Construction period 2006–2008

China Science & Technology Museum, Beijing
Competition 2005, 1st prize (without commissioning)
Design Meinhard von Gerkan and Stephan Schütz with Stephan Rewolle
Design team Katrin Kanus, Ralf Sieber, Bin Zhou, Peng Du, David Schenke, Chun Song Dong, Na Zhang, Liu Leyi, Liu Zhihui, Iris Belle, Beidi Meng
Client Chinese Science Technology Institute
Gross floor area 105,000 m²

Development and Data Processing Center of Shanghai Futures Exchange, Shanghai-Pudong
Competition 2005
Design Meinhard von Gerkan with Magdalene Weiß
Partners Nikolaus Goetze, Wei Wu
Design team Annika Schröder, Eazy Lin, Yi Wang, Yingzhe Wang, Hung-Wei Shu, Jan Stecher, Tao Wang, Na Shen
Client Shanghai Futures Exchange
Gross floor area 80,000 m²

Hongqiao Railway Station, Shanghai
Competition 2005
Design Meinhard von Gerkan
Partner Jürgen Hillmer
Design team Evelyn Pasdzierny, Alexandra Kühne, Tilo Günther, Eduard Kaiser, Markus Carlsen
Client Shanghai Railway Administration
Gross floor area 260,000 m²

New World Center, Beijing
Competition 2005, 1st prize
Design Meinhard von Gerkan and Stephan Schütz
Design team Stephan Rewolle, Le Yi Liu, Iris Belle, Bin Zhou, Zhihui Liu
Gross floor area 31,700 m²

Huawei Software Park, Nanjing
Research and Development Center
Consultancy 2005, 2nd rank
Design Meinhard von Gerkan and Stephan Schütz
Design team Giuseppina Orto, Stephan Rewolle Tobias Keyl, Xin Meng, Kian Lian, David Schenke
Client Huawei Technologies Co., Ltd.
Gross floor area 347,500 m²

Dahongmen Area, Beijing
Consultancy 2005
Design Meinhard von Gerkan and Stephan Schütz
Design team Stephan Rewolle, Giuseppina Orto, Ralf Sieber, Katrin Kanus
Client Beijing Zhujiang Huabei Zhiye Co., Ltd.
Gross floor area 1,946,000 m²

Digital TV Station, Tianjin
Competition 2005
Design Meinhard von Gerkan with Stephan Schütz and Stephan Rewolle
Design team Beidi Meng, Zhihui Liu, Di Wu, Peng Du, Na Zhang, Bin Zhou, Ralf Sieber, Patrick Pfleiderer, Katina Roloff, Iris Belle
Client Tianjin Disai
Construction & Engineering Design Service Co., Ltd.
Gross floor area 200,000 m²

Headquarters of Zhejiang Wuchan Group, Hangzhou
Consultancy 2005, 1st rank
Design Meinhard von Gerkan with Hinrich Müller
Partner Nikolaus Goetze
Project manager Volkmar Sievers
Design team Katrin Loeser, Flori Jackowski, Matthias Mumm

Project team Nils Dethlefs, Diana Spanier, Wiebke Meyenburg, Inga Kläschen
Chinese partner practice ZADRI, Zhejiang Architecture Design and Research Institute
Client Zhejiang Materials Industry Property Co., Ltd.
Gross floor area 12,700 m²
Construction period 2007–2009

Management Center of the Shanghai Free Trade Port
Design Meinhard von Gerkan, 2005
Partner Nikolaus Goetze
Project management Jörn Ortmann
Design team Hung-Wei Hsu, Yunping Ren
Chinese partner practice SIADR
Client Shanghai Lingang International Logistics Development Co., Ltd.
Gross floor area 327,000 m²
Construction period 2006–2008

Park Lights, Lingang New City
Design Meinhard von Gerkan with Magdalene Weiß and Yingzhe Wang, 2005
Chinese partner practice Zumtobel China
Client Shanghai Harbour City Development (Group) Co., Ltd.
Construction period 2005

Façade Design of High Tech Park, Heavy Industry Zone, Lingang
Design Meinhard von Gerkan with Magdalene Weiß, 2005
Partner Nikolaus Goetze
Design and project team Jan Stecher, Yingzhe Wang, Peng Xiangge, Tao Wang, Na Shen
Client Shanghai Caohejing High Tech Park New Economic Zone Development Co., Ltd.
Gross floor area 196,000 m²
Construction period 2006–2007

Twin Towers, Taihu Plaza, Wuxi
Competition 2005
Design Meinhard von Gerkan
Partner Nikolaus Goetze
Project team Volkmar Sievers, Jan Stolte, Nils Dethlefs, Tilo Günther, Andrea Moritz, Wiebke Meyenburg, Christian Krüger
Client Wuxi Planning Bureau, Wuxi Daily Press Group, Wuxi Radio and TV Bureau
Gross floor area 272,300 m²

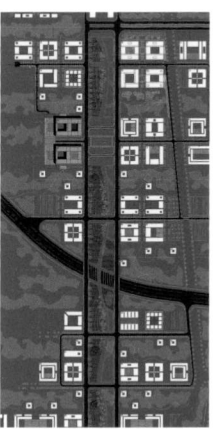

**China Telecom, Buildings
3 & 4, Shanghai**
Operation and
administration buildings
Competition 2005
Design Meinhard von Gerkan
and Nikolaus Goetze
Design team Dirk Heller,
Karen Schroeder, Christoph
Berle, Friedhelm Chlosta,
Hung-Wei Hsu, Meike
Schmidt, Holger Schmücker,
Kai Siebke, Georg Traun,
Di Wu
Client China Telecom
Shanghai
Gross floor area 42,000 m²

**Science City Culture and
Entertainment Center,
Guangzhou**
Competition 2005
Design Meinhard von Gerkan
and Stephan Schütz
Design team Christian
Dorndorf, Nicolas Pomränke,
Giuseppina Orto, Meng Xin,
Lian Kian, Ji Xu, Clemens
Kampermann, Tobias Keyl
Client Comitee of
Architectural Design
Competition by Invitation for
Guangzhou Science City
Culture and Entertainment
Center
Gross floor area 90,000 m²

**China Telecom, Buildings
12 & 13, Shanghai**
Telecommunication
equipment building and
administration building
Competition 2005, 1st prize
Design Meinhard von Gerkan
Partner Nikolaus Goetze
Project management
Dirk Heller, Karen Schroeder
Design and project team
Meike Schmidt, Friedhelm
Chlosta, Christoph Berle,
Georg Traun, Holger
Schmücker, Di Wu
Chinese partner practice
China Information Technology
Designing & Consulting
Institute
Client China Telecom
Shanghai
Gross floor area 50,000 m²
Construction period
2005–2007

**Cosco Jiangtai Project,
Beijing**
Design Meinhard von Gerkan
and Nikolaus Goetze, 2005
Design team Dirk Heller,
Karen Schroeder, Christoph
Berle, Meike Schmidt, Holger
Schmücker, Friedhelm Chlosta,
Kai Siebke, Georg Traun
Client Cosco Real Estate
Development Co.

**Archetype Building Block
at the New Bund, Lingang
New City**
Consultancy 2005
Design Meinhard von Gerkan
Design team Evelyn
Pasdzierny, Alexandra Kühne
Client Shanghai Harbourcity
Investment Co.
Gross floor area 80,000 m²

Hou Pu Office, Beijing
Design Meinhard von Gerkan
and Stephan Schütz with
Stephan Rewolle, 2005
Design team Katina Roloff,
Peng Du, Bin Zhou, David
Schenke
Client Beijing Houpu
Estate Co.
Gross floor area 150,000 m²

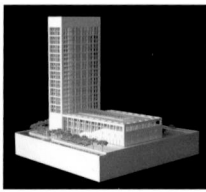

**Xiaoshan Electricity
Dispatch Building,
Hangzhou**
Competition 2005
Design Meinhard von Gerkan
Design team Volkmar
Sievers, Simone Nentwig, Tilo
Günther, Uli Rösler, Jana
Bormann
Client Xiaoshan Electricity
Dispach Building Working
Group + Zhejiang Zhongxin
Electrical Group Properties
Co., Ltd.

Taihu New Town, Wuxi
Competition 2005
Design Meinhard von Gerkan
Partner Nikolaus Goetze
Design team Marc Ziemons,
Hinrich Müller, Christiane
Fickers, Christian Dahle, Flori
Jackowski, Katrin Loeser,
Richard Sprenger
Client Wuxi Planning Bureau
Area 9,300 m²

**China Telecom, Buildings
16a & 16b, Shanghai**
Teaching and training and
dormitory building
Competition 2005, 1st prize
Design Meinhard von Gerkan
and Nikolaus Goetze
Project managers Dirk
Heller, Karen Schroeder
Project team Christoph Berle,
Friedhelm Chlosta, Meike
Schmidt, Holger Schmücker,
Kai Siebke, Georg Traun,
Katharina Traupe, Di Wu
Chinese partner practice
China Information Technology
Designing & Consulting
Institute
Client China Telecom
Shanghai
Gross floor area 25,000 m²
Construction period
2006–2008

**Pazhou Exhibition Center,
Guangzhou**
Competition 2006
Design Meinhard von Gerkan
with Marc Ziemons
Partner Nikolaus Goetze
Design team Katrin Loeser,
Henning Fritsch, Heiko Thiess,
Flori Jackowski, Kristina Milani,
Christine von der Schulen-
burg
Client China Foreign Trade
Center
Gross floor area
230,000 m²

Newmart Plaza, Harbin
Competition 2006
Design Meinhard von Gerkan
and Stephan Schütz
Project team David Schenke,
Linlin Jiang, Iris Belle, Na
Zhang, Chunsong Dong, Peng
Du, Difei Yao, Bin Zhou
Gross floor area 100,000 m²

**Stock Exchange Towers,
Shenzhen**
Competition 2006
Design Meinhard von Gerkan
Partners Nikolaus Goetze,
Wei Wu
Design team Volkmar
Sievers, Simone Nentwig, Tilo
Günther, Jan Stolte, Jana
Bormann, Alexandra Kühne,
Uli Rösler, Nils Dethlefs,
Andrea Moritz
Gross floor area 217,560m²

**China Mobile Operation
Center, Beijing**
Competition 2006, 1st prize
Design Meinhard von Gerkan
and Stephan Schütz with
Nicolas Pomränke
Design team Ralf Sieber,
Meng Xin, Lian Kian, Patrick
Pfleiderer, Bin Zhou
Project team David Schenke,
Xiao Peng, Ran Li, Mehrafarin
Ruzbehi
Chinese partner practice
Hongdu Architecture Institute
Client China Mobile,
represented by Beijing
Science Park Auction &
Tender Co., Ltd.
Gross floor area 150,000 m²
At planning stage

**Water Feature & Central
Area of Guangzhou
Science Center**
Competition 2006
Design Meinhard von Gerkan
and Stephan Schütz with
Nicolas Pomränke
Design team Christian
Dorndorf, Meng Xin, Lian Kian,
Tobias Keyl, Giuseppina Orto,
Johannes Erdmann
Gross floor area
Water Feature 15,500 m²,
GSC Center 87,100 m²

ICBC Business Operation Center, Beijing
Competition 2006
Design Meinhard von Gerkan and Stephan Schütz with Stephan Rewolle
Design team Katina Roloff, Iris Belle, Lan Chen, Difei Yao, Bin Zhou, Peng Du, Patrick Pfleiderer Lin, Xia
Client Project Office for ICBC Business Operation Center
Gross floor area 100,000 m²

Pujiang Loft Complex for Multipurpose Use, Shanghai
Design Meinhard von Gerkan with Magdalene Weiß and Jan Stecher, 2006
Partner Nikolaus Goetze
Design and project team Viktor Oldiges, Susanne Maijer, Peng Xiangge, Tan Tian, Zhou Yunkai
Chinese partner practice Shanghai XianDai HuaGai Institute of Architectural Design & Research Co., Ltd.
Client Shanghai Caohejing Development Area Economic and Technology Development Co., Ltd.
Gross floor area 145,000 m²
Construction period 2006–2008

Shanghai Business Park
Design Meinhard von Gerkan, 2006
Partner Nikolaus Goetze
Project management Magdalene Weiß, Fanny Hoffmann-Loss
Design team Yi Ling, Yajing Sun
Chinese partner practice SIMEE
Client Cao He Jing Group
Gross floor area 82,000 m²
Construction period 2007–2008

Technic Center "Freetrade II", Lingang Administration building
Competition 2006, 1st prize
Design Meinhard von Gerkan
Partner Nikolaus Goetze
Project management Klaus Lenz
Design team Udo Meyer, Matthias Mumm, Eduard Kaiser, Richard Sprenger
Project team Matthias Holtschmidt, Marcus Tanzen, Frederik Heisel, Jens Reichert, Honghao Zhu
Chinese partner practice SIADR
Client Shanghai Lingang International Logistics Development Co., Ltd.
Gross floor area 35,000 m²
Construction period 2006–2007

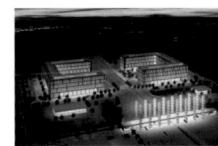

Airport Logistics Public Service Center, Shanghai
Competition 2006, 1st prize
Design Meinhard von Gerkan
Partner Nikolaus Goetze
Project management Jan Blasko and Magdalene Weiß
Design team Evelyn Pasdzierny, Hinrich Müller, Jessica Last
Project team Kornelius Kohlmeyer, Chonghan Zhao, Yunkai Zhou, Xia Hua
Chinese partner practice DRC
Client Shanghai Pudong Advanced Industry Development Co. Ltd.
Gross floor area 93,400 m²
Construction period 2007–2008

Brands Exhibition Plaza, Jinjiang
Competition 2006, 3rd prize
Design Volkwin Marg
Partner Nikolaus Goetze
Design team Marc Ziemons, Heiko Thiess, Christiane Fickers, Henning Fritsch, Monika van Vught
Client Jinjiang Government: Jinjiang Exhibition Affair Co., Ltd.
Gross floor area 140,000 m²

Ministry of Commerce, Phase II, Beijing
Competition 2006
Design Meinhard von Gerkan and Stephan Schütz
Design team Stephan Rewolle, Katina Roloff, Iris Belle, Lin Xia, Chunsong Dong, Peng Du, Patrick Pfleiderer
Gross floor area 70,000 m²

The Laboratory Complex of Liaoning Entry-Exit Inspection and Quarantine Bureau, Dalian
Competition 2006, 1st prize
Design Meinhard von Gerkan and Nikolaus Goetze
Design team Dirk Heller, Evelyn Pasdzierny, Alexandra Kühne, Tilo Günther
Client Construction Office of Liaoning Entry-Exit Inspection and Quarantine Bureau
Gross floor area 56,000 m²

Finance Street, Plot A2/8, Beijing
Study 2006
Design Meinhard von Gerkan and Stephan Schütz
Design team Ralf Sieber, Clemens Kampermann, Ji Xu, Lian Kian
Client Financial Street Control Stock Co., Ltd.
Gross floor area 124,400 m²

Qingdao Towers
Competition 2006, 1st prize
Design Meinhard von Gerkan and Stephan Schütz with Nicolas Pomränke
Design team Clemens Kampermann, Tobias Keyl, Lian Kian, Meng Xin, Giuseppina Orto, Ralf Sieber, Xu Ji
Chinese partner practice Beijang Design Group
Client Qingdao Zhongjin Yuneng Properties Co., Ltd.
Gross floor area 420,000 m²
At planning stage

Guangzhou TV Station
Competition 2006, 1st prize
Design Meinhard von Gerkan and Stephan Schütz with Stephan Rewolle
Design team Iris Belle, David Schenke, Na Zhang, Linlin Jiang, Chunsong Dong, Bin Zhou, Di Wu
Client Guangzhou TV Station
Gross floor area 319,000 m²
Construction period 2008–2010

International Conference and Exhibition Center, Xi'an
Competition 2006, 1st prize
Design Volkwin Marg
Partner Nikolaus Goetze
Project managers Hinrich Müller, Marc Ziemons
Design and project team Christine von der Schulenburg, Andreas Jantzen, Ben Grope, Tanja Gutena, Carsten Plog, Mei Pan, Honghao Zhu, Alexandra Kühne, Stephan Berndt, Zhengao Li
Structural engineers Sobek Ingenieure
Technical building equipment IGTech
Lighting design AG Licht
Landscape design Breimann & Bruun
Chinese partner practice Architectural Design & Research Inst.
South China University of Technology (SCUT)
Client Xi'an Qujiang Cultural Industry Investment Group
AHB Architectural Design & Engineering Ltd.
Gross floor area 152,000 m²
Construction period 2006–2007

Yue Tan South Street, Beijing
Administrative complex
Consultancy 2006
Design Meinhard von Gerkan and Stephan Schütz with Stephan Rewolle
Design team Katina Roloff, Peng Du, Patrick Pfleiderer, Bin Zhou, Iris Belle
Client Financial Street Control Stock Co., Ltd.
Gross floor area 80,000 m²

Taihu Administration Center, Wuxi
Competition 2006, 1st prize
Design Meinhard von Gerkan and Stephan Schütz
Design team Tobias Keyl, Christian Dorndorf, Alexander Niederhaus, Kuno von Häfen, Lian Kian, Meng Xin, Kati Mutschlechner
Client Town of Wuxi
Gross floor area
urban planning 1,738,000 m², administration center 335,000 m²
Construction beginning 2007

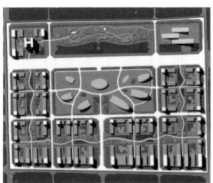

Core Zone of South New Area, Chengdu City
Competition 2006
Design Meinhard von Gerkan
Partner Nikolaus Goetze
Design team Klaus Lenz, Jessica Last, Richard Sprenger

Yue Tan North Street, Beijing
Consultancy 2006
Design Meinhard von Gerkan and Stephan Schütz with Stephan Rewolle
Design team Katina Roloff, Lan Chen, Peng Du, Bin Zhou
Client Financial Street Control Stock Co., Ltd.
Gross floor area 438,000 m²

Qingdao International Finance Plaza
Competition 2006, 1st prize
Design Meinhard von Gerkan and Stephan Schütz with Nicolas Pomränke
Project management Nicolas Pomränke, Clemens Kampermann
Design and project team Lian Kian, Ling Li, Feng Xie, Annette Löber, Amelie Neusen, Tobias Keyl, Jochen Sültrup, Meng Xin
Chinese partner practice CABR
Client Qingdao Wanzhengtong Properties Ltd.
Gross floor area 127,000 m²
Construction period 2007–2009

Qianjiang New City, Plot 43, Hangzhou
Five high-rise buildings
Competition 2006, 1st prize
Design Meinhard von Gerkan with Heiko Thiess
Partner Nikolaus Goetze
Project management Dirk Heller, Heiko Thiess
Design and team Dirk Seyffert, Katrin Loeser, Henning Fritsch, Christian Dahle
Chinese partner practice ZIAD
Client Hangzhou Jinji Real Estate Development Co., Ltd.
Gross floor area 139,000 m²
Construction period 2008–2012

Taiyuan Changfeng Culture Business Area
Competition 2006
Design Meinhard von Gerkan and Stephan Schütz
Design team David Schenke, Lin Lin Jiang, Katina Roloff, Bin Zhou, Peng Du
Client Dalian Wanda Group
Gross floor area 2,575,400 m²

TEDA Residential Area, Tianjin
Ten residential areas
Competition 2006, 1st prize
Design Meinhard von Gerkan and Stephan Schütz
Design team Stephan Rewolle, Katina Roloff, Iris Belle, Lan Chen, Yan Liu, Patrick Pfleiderer, Bin Zhou, Yue Wang, Jun Li, Lu Han
Client TEDA Construction and Development Bureau
Gross floor area 1,648,000 m²

Olympic Sports Center, Shenzhen
Competition 2006, 1st prize
Design Meinhard von Gerkan and Stephan Schütz with Nicolas Pomränke
Project management Ralf Sieber
Design and project team Ji Xu, Alexander Niederhaus, Cheng Huang, Marlene Törper, Niklas Veelken, Martin Gänsicke, Stephanie Brendel, Andrea Moritz, Xin Zheng, Semra Ugur, Kralyu Chobanov, Christian Dorndorf, Lian Kian, Bin Zhou, Tobias Keyl, Li Ling, Helge Lezius, Xin Meng, Kuno von Haefen, Kathi Mutschlechner
Chinese partner practices SADI, CNADRI, CCDI, BLY
Client SHENZHEN WORKS BUREAU, Bureau of Public Works of Shenzhen Municipality

Site area 870,000 m²
Stadium 60,000 seats
Multifunctional hall 18,000 seats
Swimming hall 3,000 seats
Construction period 2007–2010

Central Area of Nanshan Cultural & Sports Center
Competition 2006, 1st prize
Design Meinhard von Gerkan and Stephan Schütz with Nicolas Pomränke
Design team Giuseppina Orto, Clemens Kampermann, Lian Kian, Ralf Sieber, Christian Dorndorf, Alexander Niederhaus, Li Ling
Client Nanshan Municipal Government of Shenzhen
Gross floor area 44,000 m²

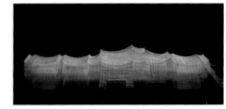

Public Event Center for the World Expo 2010, Shanghai
Competition 2006
Design Meinhard von Gerkan
Partner Nikolaus Goetze
Design team Volkmar Sievers, Magdalene Weiß, Silke Jessen, Christian Krüger, Diana Spanier, Julia Krüger, Alexandra Kühne, Huan Zhu, Kerstin Steinfatt, Jana Bormann, Tilo Günther, Rouven Oberdiek, Andrea Moritz, Nils Dethlefs, Kornelius Kohlmeyer, Arndt Weiß, Honghao Zhu, Jan Blasko, Alexander Schober, Chen Fu, Chonghan Zhao, Cha Lu, Yuqi Mao, Viktor Oldiges
Client Shanghai World Expo (Group) Co., Ltd.

Wenyang Auto Fittings Development & Testing Building, Shanghai
Competition 2006, 1st prize
Design Meinhard von Gerkan and Nikolaus Goetze with Annika Schröder
Project management Magdalene Weiß
Design team Evelyn Pasdzierny, Ben Grope, Huang Weiyi
Project team Alexander Schober, Cha Lu, Jan Blasko, Xia Hua, Yunhai Zho
Chinese partner practice SIMEE
Client Shanghai Wenyang Science & Technology Development Co., Ltd.
Gross floor area 35,000 m²
Construction period 2008–2009

China Mobile South Base, Guangzhou
Competition 2006, 1st prize
Design Meinhard von Gerkan
Partner Nikolaus Goetze
Project management Volkmar Sievers

Design and project team
Silke Jessen, Julia Wegner,
Jan Stolte, Christian Dahle,
Uli Rösler, Tilo Günther,
Nils Dethlefs, Philipp
Lehmann, Gabi Nunnemann,
Jana Bormann, Simone
Nentwig, Wiebke Meyenburg,
Diana Spanier, Christian
Krüger
Structural engineers
Sobek Ingenieure
Chinese partner practice
GZPI
Client China Mobile
Gross floor area 165,000 m²
Construction period
2007–2009

**Sanya Beauty Town,
Hainan**
**Urban design with musical
theater**
Competition 2006
Design Meinhard von Gerkan
Partner Nikolaus Goetze
Design team Annika
Schröder, Marcus Tanzen,
Udo Meyer, Dirk Seyffert,
Jessica Last
Client Hainan Sanya Bay New
Town Development Co. Ltd.
Gross floor area
188,000 m²,
musical theater 34,700 m²

**Airport Logistic Zone and
Industrial Biotech Base,
Tianjin**
Competition 2006, 1st prize
Design Meinhard von Gerkan
and Stephan Schütz
Project management Doris
Schäffler
Design team Tobias Keyl,
Stephan Rewolle, Kuno von
Häfen, Alexander Niederhaus,
Nicolas Pomränke, Meng Xin,
Ling Li, Lian Kian, Kathi
Mutschlechner
Chinese partner practice
CABR
Client Tianjin Airport Logistic
Zone Committee
Gross floor area 44,500 m²
Construction period
2007–2008

**East New City CBD, Site
B14/B15, Ningbo**
Three high-rise buildings
Competition 2006
Design Meinhard von Gerkan
Partner Nikolaus Goetze
Design team Tilo Günther,
Andrea Moritz, Christian
Krüger
Client Ningbo Port Group;
Ningbo East New City
Development & Construction
Headquarter
Gross floor area
187,000 m²

**West Lake Science Park,
Hangzhou**
Urban planning
Competition 2006
Design Meinhard von Gerkan
Partner Nikolaus Goetze
Design team Volkmar
Sievers, Tilo Günther, Jan
Stolte, Alexandra Kühne, Julia
Wegner
Client Canhigh Estate Group
Co., Ltd.

**Huawei Environmental
Protection Park, Beijing**
Competition 2006
Design Meinhard von Gerkan
and Stephan Schütz with
Nicolas Pomränke
Design team Christian
Dorndorf, Bernd Gotthardt,
Lian Kian, Clemens
Kampermann, Jochen Sültrup,
Kuno von Häfen, Stephan
Rewolle, Katina Roloff, David
Schenke, Lan Chen, Yan Liu,
Bin Zhou, Jiantong Zhao, Yue
Wang, Jun Li
Client Huawei Technologies
Co., Ltd.
Gross floor area 104,200 m²
(above ground)
At planning stage

**Qujiang International
Conference and Exhibition
Center, Xi'an**
Urban planning
Consultancy 2006
Design Volkwin Marg with
Hinrich Müller and Marc
Ziemons
Partner Nikolaus Goetze
Design team Annika
Schröder, Kristina Gerdt, Ben
Grope, Andreas Jantzen,
Eduard Kaiser, Mei Pan,
Honghao Zhu
Client AHB
Gross floor area
1,770,000 m²

ChinaPetrol, Dalian
Office building
Competition 2006,
1st prize group
Design Meinhard von Gerkan
and Stephan Schütz with
Nicolas Pomränke
Design team Ralf Sieber,
Clemens Kampermann, Kuno
von Häfen, Alexander
Niederhaus
Client PetroChina Dalian
Sales Branch Company
Gross floor area 75,000 m²

**Basketball Center,
Dongguan**
Competition 2006, 1st prize
Design Meinhard von Gerkan
and Stephan Schütz
Project management
Stephan Rewolle

Design team Katina Roloff,
Patrick Pfleiderer, Matthias
Wiegelmann, Chunsong Dong,
Bin Zhou, Yan Liu, Yue Wang,
Jun Li, Lu Han, Ping Cao,
Linda Stannieder, Li Yang,
Chaojie Yin
Structural engineers
Schlaich, Bergermann and
Partners
Chinese partner practice
CABR
Client Dongguan Civil
Construction Administration
Office
Gross floor area 60,600 m²
Seats 14,730
Construction period
2006–2009

**Shandong Provincial
Museum, Ji'nan**
Competition 2006
Design Meinhard von Gerkan
and Stephan Schütz with
Stephan Rewolle
Design team Iris Belle,
Patrick Pfleiderer, Katina
Roloff, Yan Liu, Jiantong Zhao,
Chunsong Dong, Yu Wang, Jun
Li, David Schenke, Di Wu, Bin
Zhou
Gross floor area 80,000 m²

**Public Library, Shanghai-
Pudong**
Competition 2006
Design Meinhard von Gerkan
Partner Nikolaus Goetze
Design team Klaus Lenz,
Diana Bunic, Jessica Last,
Marcus Tanzen, Udo Meyer
Client SITC Shanghai
International Tendering Co.,
Ltd.
Gross floor area 66,400 m²

**Performance Art Center,
Expo 2010, Shanghai**
Competition 2006/2007
Design Meinhard von Gerkan
Partner Nikolaus Goetze
Design team Evelyn
Pasdzierny, Alexandra Kühne,
Kerstin Steinfatt, Jan Stolte,
Silke Jessen, Ingo Beckmann,
Christian Dahle, Eduard Kaiser,
Magdalene Weiß, Susanne
Maijer, Chen Fu, Qing Wang,
Yan Zhang, Honghao Zhu
Client Shanghai Culture Radio
Film TV Group
Gross floor area 80,000 m²

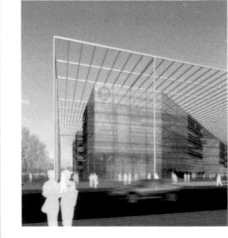

**Credit Card Center, China
Merchants Bank, Shanghai**
Competition 2006
Design Meinhard von Gerkan
Partner Nikolaus Goetze
Design team Klaus Lenz,
Richard Sprenger, Udo Meyer,
Matthias Mumm, Kostadin
Kochev
Client CMB Bank, Shenzhen
Gross floor area
130,300 m²

Information Center, Lingang
Competition 2006, 1st prize
Design Meinhard von Gerkan
Partner Nikolaus Goetze
Project management Magdalene Weiß, Jan Blasko
Design and project team Honghao Zhu, Susanne Maijer, Yunkai Zhou, Kornelius Kohlmeyer, Claudius Lange, Arndt Weiß
Client Lingang Development Group
Gross floor area 36,000 m²
Construction period 2008–2009

Baosteel Headquarters, Shanghai
Consultancy 2006
Design Meinhard von Gerkan
Partner Nikolaus Goetze
Design team Hinrich Müller, Marc Ziemons, Heiko Thiess, Christine von der Schulenburg, Andreas Jantzen, Ben Grope, Dirk Seyffert, Mei Pan
Gross floor area 100,000 m²

Shimao New City, Jiaxing, Shanghai
Urban planning
Competition 2006
Design Meinhard von Gerkan
Partner Nikolaus Goetze
Design team Klaus Lenz, Diana Bunic, Jessica Last, Hua Fang
Client Shimao Group
Gross floor area 879,000 m²

Port Inspection and Logistic Center, Xiamen
Competition 2006, 2nd prize
Design Meinhard von Gerkan and Stephan Schütz with Nicolas Pomränke
Design team Christian Dorndorf, Lian Kian, Clemens Kampermann, Ralf Sieber, Ji Xu, Meng Xin, Jochen Sültrup, Bin Zhou
Client Xiamen Port Joint Inspection and Logistic Operation Center Dev. Co., Ltd.
Gross floor area 138,000 m²

Ping An Plaza, Shenzhen
High-rise building
Competition 2006, 1st prize
Design Meinhard von Gerkan
Partners Nikolaus Goetze, Wei Wu
Design team Magdalene Weiß, Annika Schröder, Kristina Gerdt, Sigrid Müller, Yunping Ren, Lei Cai
Client Ping An Insurance (Group) Company of China, Ltd.
Gross floor area 120,000 m²

Club and Spa Building, Lingang
Design Meinhard von Gerkan, 2006
Partner Nikolaus Goetze
Project management Jan Blasko and Magdalene Weiß
Design team Claudius Lange, Yunkai Zhou
Chinese partner practice SIMEE
Client Lingang Development Group
Gross floor area 10,200 m² (aboveground)
Construction period 2008–2009

Museum for Culture, Fine Arts and Science, Changchun
Competition 2006, 1st prize
Design Meinhard von Gerkan
Partner Nikolaus Goetze
Project management Hinrich Müller, Marc Ziemons
Design and project team Christine von der Schulenburg, Andreas Jantzen, Katrin Loeser, Sven Grotheer, Katja Siebke, Kristina Milani, Tanja Gutena, Heiko Thiess, Dirk Seyffert, Pan Mei, Anna Rzymelka, Ben Grope, Markus Carlsen
Chinese partner practice JPADI, Jilin Provincial Architecture Design Institute Co., Ltd.
Client Changchun Science and Culture Center Project Leading Team
Gross floor area 107,500 m²
Construction period 2007–2009

Poly Plaza, Shanghai-Pudong
Shopping mall, office and apartment complex
Competition 2006, 1st prize
Design Meinhard von Gerkan with Magdalene Weiß
Partners Nikolaus Goetze, Wei Wu
Project managers Alexander Schober, Hao Yan Li, Annika Schröder
Design team Yi Wang, Eazy Lin, Yingzhe Wang, Jan Stecher, Jörn Ortmann
Project team Jing Hai Tian, Yu Qi Mao, Jan Blasko, Yan Li Hao, Chen Fu
Chinese partner practice ECADI
Client Shanghai Poly Xin Real Estate Co., Ltd.
Gross floor area 100,000 m²
Construction period 2007–2009

Siemens Center, Shanghai,
Competition 2006, 1st prize
Design Meinhard von Gerkan and Nikolaus Goetze with Klaus Lenz
Project management Jörn Ortmann
Design and project team Frederik Heisel, Honghao Zhu, Udo Meyer, Marcus Tanzen, Matthias Mumm, Christian Dahle, Stephan Seeger, Bin Zhou
Chinese partner practice SIADR
Client Siemens Real Estate (SRE) and Siemens Ltd. China (SLC)
Gross floor area 110,000 m²
Construction period 2007–2009

Baijiazhuang Xili Project, Beijing
Office and commercial building
Competition 2006, 1st prize
Design Meinhard von Gerkan and Stephan Schütz
Project management Nicolas Pomränke
Design and project team Johannes Erdmann, Torsten Bessel, Semra Ugur, Ralf Sieber, Ji Xu, Christian Dorndorf
Chinese partner practice CABR
Client Jia Ming Investment (Group) Co., Ltd.
Beijing Hengshi Huarong Real Estate Development Co., Ltd.
Gross floor area 90,500 m²
Construction period 2008–2009

Hopson Desheng Tower, Beijing
Office tower with commercial areas
Design Meinhard von Gerkan and Stephan Schütz, 2007
Project manager David Schenke
Design team Lin Lin Jiang, Daniela Franz, Ran Li, Bin Zhou, Yang Liu
Chinese partner practice Meixin Architecture Design Company
Client Hopson Property Development Group
Gross floor area 57,300 m²
At planning stage

Huawei Development & Research Office Buildings, Shenzhen
Design Meinhard von Gerkan and Stephan Schütz with Stephan Rewolle, 2007
Design team Katina Roloff, Li Yang, Linda Stannieder, Chao Jie Yin, Fei Zheng, Bin Zhou
Chinese partner practice SIADR

Client Huawei Technologies Co., Ltd.
Gross floor area 226,000 m²
At planning stage

Poly Theater, Changchun
Competition 2007
Design Meinhard von Gerkan
Partner Nikolaus Goetze
Design team Evelyn Pasdzierny, Alexandra Kühne, Ingo Beckmann, Eduard Kaiser, Van-Hai Ngyuen
Client Poly Real Estate Group Co.
Gross floor area 42,000 m²

GDA Plaza, Hangzhou
Competition 2007, 1st prize
Design Meinhard von Gerkan
Partner Nikolaus Goetze
Project management Magdalene Weiß
Design and project team Jan Blasko, Jörn Ortmann, Lei Cai, Honghao Zhu, Ying Chen, Yi Jiang, Yajin Sun, Chonghan Zhao, Yi Jiang, Claudius Lange, Alexander Schober, Jinghai Tian, Yuqi Mao
Chinese partner practice ZADRI
Client GDA Group
Gross floor area 107,000 m²
Construction period 2007–2009

Huawei Software Company, Chengdu
Consultancy 2007
Design Meinhard von Gerkan and Stephan Schütz with Nicolas Pomränke
Design team Bernd Gotthardt, Christian Dorndorf, Lian Kian, Clemens Kampermann, Jochen Sültrup, Kuno von Häfen
Project team Christian Dorndorf, Meng Xin, Yuqing Kang
Client Huawei Technologies Co., Ltd.
Gross floor area 280,000 m²
At planning stage

Business and Trade Center, Shenzhen
Competition 2007
Design Meinhard von Gerkan
Partner Nikolaus Goetze
Design team Klaus Lenz, Jessica Last, Hua Fang, Van-Hai Nguyen
Client Yangfu Industrial (Shenzhen) Co., Ltd.
Gross floor area 216,000 m²

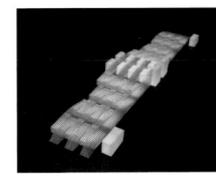

Coal Trade Center, Taiyuan
Competition 2007
Design Volkwin Marg
Partner Nikolaus Goetze
Design team Marc Ziemons, Monika van Vught, Nana Apel, Heiko Thiess, Dirk Seyffert, Theresa Jonetzki
Client Shanxi Provincial Coal Transportation & Sale Corporation
Gross floor area 189,500 m²

Hotel South Island, Lingang
Competition 2007
Design Meinhard von Gerkan
Partner Nikolaus Goetze
Design team Evelyn Pasdzierny, Alexandra Kühne, Christian Krüger, Eduard Kaiser, Ingo Beckmann, Van-Hai Nguyen
Client Shanghai Gangcheng Dev. (Group) Co., Ltd.
Gross floor area 40,000 m²

Urban Design for Bund Waterfront, Shanghai
Competition 2007/2008
Design Meinhard von Gerkan
Partner Nikolaus Goetze
Project management Magdalene Weiß
Design team Rebekka Brauer, Honghao Zhu, Yi Lin, Chen Fu, Hendrik Wings, Qing Wang, Susanne Maijer, Rui Kong
Client Shanghai Urban Planning & Administration Bureau
Length 3,300 m

TEDA Theater, Tianjin
Competition 2007
Design Meinhard von Gerkan and Stephan Schütz with Nicolas Pomränke
Design team Clemens Kampermann, Kian Lian
Client Construction Development Bureau of TEDA Administrative Commission
Gross floor area 51,100 m²

B2-10 Tower, Guangzhou Office building
Competition 2007
Design Meinhard von Gerkan
Partner Nikolaus Goetze
Design team Heiko Thiess, Dirk Heller, Dirk Seyffert, Christoph Berle, Hua Fang
Client Guangzhou City Construction and Development Co., Ltd.
Gross floor area 172,300 m²

Bao'an International Airport, Terminal 3, Shenzhen
Competition 2007
Design Meinhard von Gerkan
Partner Nikolaus Goetze
Design team Volkmar Sievers, Christian Dahle, Jan Stolte, Julia Wegner, Deren Akdeniz, Tom Schülke, Markus Carlsen, Eduard Kaiser, Ingo Beckmann, Nils Dethlefs, Uli Rösler, Jana Bormann, Kerstin Steinfatt
Client Shenzhen Airport (Group) Co., Ltd.
Gross floor area 464,000 m²

1st Finance and Business District of Taihu New City, Wuxi
Consultancy 2007
Design Meinhard von Gerkan and Stephan Schütz
Project management Tobias Keyl
Design team Nicolas Pomränke, Sabine Stage, Clemens Ahlgrimm, Ben Bilz
Client Taihu Mew City Construction and Investment Management Co., Ltd.
Gross floor area 830,000 m²

Finance District B17-B21, Ningbo
Competition 2007
Design Meinhard von Gerkan
Partner Nikolaus Goetze
Design team Volkmar Sievers, Tilo Günther, Silke Jessen, Wiebke Meyenburg, Christian Krüger, Eduard Kaiser, Ingo Beckmann, Tom Schülke, Markus Carlsen
Client Ningbo East New City Development & Construction
Gross floor area 252,500 m²

Cultural Village, Huai An
Competition 2007
Design Meinhard von Gerkan and Stephan Schütz with Stephan Rewolle
Design team Daniela Franz, Christa Hillebrand, Yoko Uraji, Xi Zhang, Yang Liu, Yu Zhan, Linda Stannieder, Linlin Jiang, Bin Zhou, Chunsong Dong
Client Huai An Planning Bureau and Cultural Bureau
Gross floor area 44,000 m²

Bao'an Stadium, Shenzhen Stadium, training field, sports academy
Competition 2007, 1st prize
Design Meinhard von Gerkan and Stephan Schütz
Design team David Schenke, Jennifer Heckenlaible, Daniela Franz, Ran Li, Xi Zhang, Bin Zhou, Chao Jie Yin, Anna Bulanda-Jansen, Zhan Yu
Client The Sports Bureau of Bao'an District, Shenzhen
Gross floor area 88,500 m²
At planning stage

Pazhou Plots 1301 & 1401, Guangzhou
Competition 2007
Design Meinhard von Gerkan with Magdalene Weiß
Partners Nikolaus Goetze, Wei Wu
Design team Jörn Ortmann, Alexander Schober, Henrik Wings, Cha Lu, Qing Wang, Xia Hua, Yan Zhang
Client Nan Fung China
Gross floor area
127,600 m² (plot 1301);
143,900 m² (plot 1401)

Blocks B2 & C3, Lingang
Competition 2007
Design Meinhard von Gerkan
Partner Nikolaus Goetze
Design team Jan Blasko, Yang Xuan
Client Shanghai Gangcheng Dev. (Group) Co., Ltd.
Gross floor area
2 x 12,800 m²

Maritime Museum, Exhibition concept, Lingang New City
Competition 2007, 2nd prize
Design Meinhard von Gerkan
Partner Nikolaus Goetze
Design team Markus Tanzen, Magdalene Weiß, Lin Eazy, Xuan Yang, Yan Zhang, Mirko Buff
Client China Maritime Museum

German Pavilion for the EXPO 2010, Shanghai
Competition 2007
Design Meinhard von Gerkan
Partner Nikolaus Goetze
Design team Heiko Thiess, Dirk Seyffert
Client German Federal Ministry for Economy and Technology
Gross floor area 6,000 m²

Pujiang High Tech Park, Metro Plaza, Shanghai
Competition 2007, 1st prize
Design Meinhard von Gerkan
Partner Nikolaus Goetze
Design team Magdalene Weiß, Ying Chen, Chonghan Zhao Yi Jiang, Yajin Sun, Xuan Yang, Yan Zhang
Gross floor area
330,000 m²

PICTURE CREDITS

IMPRINT

Front cover Zhongguancun Christian Church,
photograph by Christian Gahl

© Prestel Verlag,
Munich · Berlin · London · New York 2008
von Gerkan, Marg and Partners, Hamburg

Prestel Verlag
Königinstrasse 9
80539 Munich
Tel. +49 (0)89 242908-300
Fax +49 (0)89 242908-335

Prestel Publishing Ltd.
4 Bloomsbury Place
London WC1A 2QA
Tel. +44 (0)20 7323-5004
Fax +44 (0)20 7636-8004

Prestel Publishing
900 Broadway, Suite 603
New York, N.Y. 10003
Tel. +1 (212) 995-2720
Fax +1 (212) 995-2733

www.prestel.com

Prestel books are available worldwide. Please contact your nearest
bookseller or one of the opposite addresses for information concerning
your local distributor.

The Library of Congress Cataloguing-in-Publication data is available.
British Library Cataloguing-in-Publication Data: a catalogue record for
this book is available from the British Library. The Deutsche Bibliothek
holds a record of this publication in the Deutsche Nationalbibliografie;
detailed bibliographical data can be found under: http://dnb.ddb.de

Editor Meinhard von Gerkan
Coordination Bernd Pastuschka / gmp
Text Editing ALISA – Literary Agency for Fiction and Non-Fiction
Books / Birgit Anna Lörler, Hamburg;
Editorial assistance Bettina Ahrens / gmp
Translations from the German Roderick O'Donovan, Vienna (Essay);
Murphy Translation Office, Hamburg (Projects);
Marie Frohling, Berlin (Projects)
Proof-reading Jonathan Fox, Barcelona
Design and Layout ON Grafik | Tom Wibberenz
with Nico Wolf, Hamburg
Digital Picture Editing Beatrix Hansen / gmp
Origination DZA Satz und Bild GmbH, Altenburg
Printing and Binding DZA, Druckerei zu Altenburg GmbH, Altenburg

Printed in Germany on acid-free paper

ISBN 978-3-7913-3990-0